Trade and Industrial Policy under International Oligopoly

The existence of firms with different levels of efficiency within a country plays an important role in this in-depth analysis of industrial and trade policies in a multi-country trade-theoretic framework. Sajal Lahiri and Yoshiyasu Ono examine various industrial policies, R&D subsidies and trade policies under conditions of imperfect competition in a product market created by the presence of Cournot oligopolistic interdependence in production. Trade is defined broadly to include trade in commodity as well as trade in capital, specifically foreign direct investment. While the first part of the book focuses on commodity trade and assumes full employment, the latter considers foreign direct investment and assumes the presence of unemployment. Given the importance of industrial policies and the prevalence of imperfect competition, together with on-going attention to theoretical issues concerning industrial economics, this research will excite interest amongst researchers, advanced students and policy makers in this field.

SAJAL LAHIRI is the Vandeveer Professor of Economics at Southern Illinois University at Carbondale, Illinois. He has published papers widely on international trade and development economics.

YOSHIYASU ONO is Professor of Economics at the Institute of Social and Economic Research, Osaka University. He is the author of numerous books and papers on industrial organization, international trade and dynamic macroeconomics.

Trade and Industrial Policy under International Oligopoly

Sajal Lahiri and Yoshiyasu Ono

CAMBRIDGE UNIVERSITY PRESS

PUBLISHED BY THE PRESS SYNDICATE OF THE UNIVERSITY OF CAMBRIDGE
The Pitt Building, Trumpington Street, Cambridge CB2 1RP, United Kingdom

CAMBRIDGE UNIVERSITY PRESS
The Edinburgh Building, Cambridge, CB2 2RU, UK
40 West 20th Street, New York, NY 10011–4211, USA
477 Williamstown Road, Port Melbourne, VIC 3207, Australia
Ruiz de Alarcón 13, 28014 Madrid, Spain
Dock House, The Waterfront, Cape Town 8001, South Africa

http://www.cambridge.org

First published 2004

Printed in the United Kingdom at the University Press, Cambridge

Typeface Plantin 10/12 pt.   *System* LaTeX 2_ε [TB]

A catalogue record for this book is available from the British Library

ISBN 0 521 77033 5 hardback

Dedicated to
Dipa Lahiri and Ichiko Ono
for their unstinting support

Contents

Figures

Tables

Preface

Our joint research began in 1986 at the Warwick Summer Workshop in the UK. We did not expect it to last this long, but it grew from strength to strength. This book is very much a product of this long research partnership between two individuals who were born within a month of each other. On the whole we worked on the basic theme of trade and industrial policy under asymmetric oligopoly, and one piece followed from another in a natural way. The book attempts to present the fruits of our research in a unified and coherent way. Many of the chapters of the book have appeared in journals: chapter 1 is based on Lahiri and Ono (1988), chapter 2 on Lahiri and Ono (1999b), chapter 4 on Lahiri and Ono (1997), chapter 5 on Lahiri and Ono (1999a), chapter 7 on Lahiri and Ono (1998a), chapter 8 on Lahiri and Ono (2003), and chapter 10 on Lahiri and Ono (1998b). Chapter 3 is based on a paper written by Ono on his own (Ono, 1990). However, those articles have been rewritten extensively, often adding new results, in order for the different chapters to fit in with each other. Moreover, we have written two of the chapters (6 and 9) specifically for this book in order to fill some gaps in our overall plan, and excluded a number of our published papers which do not fulfil the aim and objective of the book.

Over the years, we have benefited a great deal from discussions and/or comments from a large number of colleagues and students. In particular, we would like to thank Roy Bailey, Avinash Dixit, Huw Dixon, Rod Falvey, Scott Gilbert, Tatsuo Hatta, Michael Keen, Murray Kemp, Toshihiro Matsumura, Catia Montagna, Abhinay Muthoo, Kazuhiko Odaki, Dan Primont, Thomas Pugel, Pascalis Raimondos-Møller and Kotaro Suzumura. We have also gained from presenting our work at numerous conferences and seminars, not to mention comments from so many anonymous referees of journals. Detailed comments from four anonymous reviewers for the Cambridge University Press on an earlier draft of this manuscript helped us to improve the exposition substantially. To all of them we extend our deep sense of gratitude.

Our research has been supported in part by the following funding agencies: British Council, Kyoto Office; Economic and Social Research Council of the UK; Grants-in-Aid for Scientific Research, Ministry of Education, Japan; Inamori Foundation; International House of Japan; International Scientific Research Program, Ministry of Education, Japan; Japan Economics Research Foundation; Japan Foundation; Japan Foundation Endowment Committee, UK; Japan Securities Scholarship Foundation; Matsushita International Foundation; and the Royal Economic Society, UK. We are grateful to each one of them. However, a special thanks of course is due to our employing institutions, viz., University of Essex and Southern Illinois University Carbondale for Lahiri and Osaka University and Tokyo Institute of Technology for Ono. It is not just the financial support that we are indebted for: our research has been greatly influenced by the vigorous intellectual atmosphere in these institutions.

SAJAL LAHIRI
YOSHIYASU ONO

Introduction

Issues

In a typical competitive economy most policy interventions cause some distortions and thus reduce national welfare. In other words, laissez faire is the best option for the government in charge. In a real world, however, there are various preexisting distortions that introduce non-competitiveness in product and/or factor markets, and these make some interventions welfare enhancing. Oligopoly and unemployment are two common and important such examples.

In the presence of oligopoly, for example, producers, because of their market power, are able to reduce output so that they earn excess profits at the cost of a decrease in consumers' surplus.[1] Hence, it is commonly believed that a policy that encourages more competition among firms is desirable. In fact, this belief forms the backbone of most antitrust policies in the world. If as an extreme measure oligopolistic distortions can completely be removed, first-best will be achieved. In reality, however, such an extreme measure is difficult to implement for, *inter alia*, political-economic and technological reasons. We are then left in a second-best scenario and more competition may not always be welfare improving in such situations. When oligopoly and unemployment co-exist, the interactions between these two distortions may work in unexpected ways giving rise to more perverse outcomes in terms of second-best policies.

There is of course a very substantial literature on trade and industrial policies under oligopoly, both in the presence and absence of unemployment (see Brander, 1995; Helpman and Krugman, 1986, 1989 and Suzumura, 1995 for surveys of the literature).[2] However, in the bulk of

---

[1] For a lucid exposition of oligopoly theory see Dixon, 2001; Friedman, 1983; Norman and LaManna, 1992. Empirical aspects of oligopolistic industries are discussed, among others, in Bernhofen, 1998; Choe, 1999; Haskel and Scaramozzino, 1997; Krugman and Smith, 1994.

[2] Some of the more recent contributions are Agarwal and Barua, 1994; Asplund and Sandin, 1999; Bhattacharjee, 1995; Caho and Yu, 1997; Collie, 1998; Cordella, 1998; Cordella and Gabszewicz, 1997; Fine, 1999; Fung, 1995; Gatsion and Karp, 1992; Gisser

this literature firms, particularly those belonging to nationals of the same country, are assumed to be symmetric in terms of their cost structure. In contrast, in the analysis of this book an asymmetry in the marginal cost level among firms plays an important role in generating surprising results.[3] An illustration should drive the point home. Suppose that there are two firms with technology differentials. Naturally, the marginal profit rate of the more efficient firm is higher than that of the less efficient firm. Thus, a policy that restricts the minor firm's production may increase the total producers' surplus through a reallocation of production from the less efficient firm to the more efficient firm, although the total production declines, causing consumers' surplus to decrease. It will be shown in the next chapter that if the technology differential is sufficiently large then this increase in total profits may even dominate the decrease in consumers' surplus. This property can be extended to prove that monopoly may well realize higher welfare than duopoly. This can never occur under symmetric oligopoly.

Such an analysis can be extended to an international context in a very straightforward manner. In the presence of foreign firms, total surplus is shared by consumers, domestic producers and foreign producers. Since the surplus distributed to foreign producers is repatriated abroad, from the domestic country's viewpoint these firms are, for all intents and purposes, like very inefficient domestic firms (who make very low profits). Thus, a policy that reduces the foreign producers' output and raises the domestic ones' output may enhance domestic welfare by increasing domestic producers' surplus even if it decreases total output and hence reduces consumers' surplus.

The first half of this book examines these and other properties by analysing the welfare effects of various policies – trade policies such as tariffs and quotas and industrial policies such as elimination of firms, production subsidies and R&D subsidies – in various contexts, viz., a closed economy, an open economy and vertical relations between producers and sellers. It is shown, *inter alia*, that competition-promoting policies may well be welfare reducing although they increase total production.

The second half of this book deals with another distortion mentioned above, namely, unemployment. In the presence of unemployment a

---

and Sauer, 2000; Greaney, 1999; Holm, 1997; Hwang and Schulman, 1993; Ishikawa and Spencer, 1999; Klette, 1994; Kojima, 1990; Maggi, 1996; Rowthorn, 1992; Tanaka, 1992; Ushio, 2000.

[3] There is now a small literature on trade and industrial policy under asymmetric oligopoly. See, for example, Denicolò and Matteuzzi, 2000; Lahiri and Ono, 1988, 1997; Leahy and Montagna, 2001; Leahy and Neary, 2000, 2001; Neary, 1994; Ono, 1990; van Long and Soubeyran, 1997.

country may encourage more inward foreign direct investment (FDI) so as to create job opportunities. Since there is no opportunity cost of employing labour, any income paid to the workers employed by foreign firms becomes a net surplus to the host country. Thus, once a foreign firm enters, some intervention that compels it to employ more local workers benefits the host country. Local content requirements are usually imposed for this purpose. A profit tax on FDI is also beneficial to the host country. However, these policies reduce profits of foreign firms and induce them to relocate to another country, reducing job opportunities. Therefore, the host government has a balancing act to do in deciding the optimal local content and tax-subsidy policies.

The optimal combination of these policies should depend on a number of factors such as how efficient and how labor intensive foreign firms are, and the number of domestic firms that exist in the market. The interaction between oligopoly and unemployment may lead to interesting policy dilemmas. For example, an efficient foreign or domestic firm is good for consumers' surplus, but it may not be so good as far as employment creation is concerned. We shall analyse these issues under various market structures including export-oriented FDI and cross-hauling with differentiated commodities. We also extend the analysis by introducing lobbying activity by domestic agents.

Contents

The book analyses various industrial and trade policies in a multi-country trade-theoretic framework in the presence of Cournot oligopolistic interdependence in production. The existence of firms with different levels of efficiency within a country plays an important role in our analysis. We define 'trade' broadly to include trade in commodity as well as trade in capital (foreign direct investment, to be specific).

In chapter 1, we start with a closed-economy model in order to establish the importance of a particular mechanism which has been neglected in the literature. This mechanism, which was explained in the previous section, is about the reallocation of profits among asymmetric domestic firms. It is commonly believed that the exit of minor firms and policies that impair them strengthen the oligopoly position of major firms and consequently decrease national welfare. In this chapter we show that by eliminating or impairing minor firms a government can actually increase welfare, as outlined in the previous section.

Chapters 2 and 3 are two different extensions of chapter 1. Chapter 2 endogenizes marginal costs by explicitly considering R&D investments. The question of optimum R&D subsidies is analysed in the context of a two-stage asymmetric Cournot duopoly model. For the special case of symmetric duopoly, whether the firms should be subsidized in their R&D activities crucially depends on the concavity/convexity property of the demand function. It is also shown that a firm with some initial cost advantage should be subsidized in its R&D activities and the other one should be taxed. In this way, we once again obtain policy implications which cast doubt on the universal applicability of competition policies.

Chapter 3 extends the analysis of chapter 1 to an international context. The effect of restricting foreign penetration – by import quota and/or controls on FDI – on domestic and foreign welfare is examined under an oligopolistic setting. A restriction on imports or FDI lowers consumers' surplus but increases domestic producers' surplus in the host country. Comparing the two effects, we find conditions under which the restriction increases domestic total surplus. Furthermore, we show that the beneficial effect of the restriction may be so large that the host country could benefit even after compensating the foreign firms for the loss caused by the restriction.

Chapter 4 synthesizes the analyses in chapters 1 and 3 as well as a number of different results found in the literature on trade and industrial policies under oligopoly. It develops a general model that nests many of those in the existing literature on trade and industrial policies under oligopoly. It analyses the relationship between market shares and welfare under the assumption of Cournot oligopolistic interdependence in production. The model is general enough to deal with multiple countries, oligopolists with different levels of marginal costs within each country, and any distribution of world demand across countries. It is found that elimination of a 'minor' firm harms the country if the country's total production is 'very little'. However, such a policy always benefits the country if it exports the commodity. The welfare effect of production subsidies and the case of foreign ownership of firms are also discussed.

Chapters 5 and 6 extend chapter 3 in two different directions. Chapter 5 considers the trade aspect of chapter 3 and extends the model to allow for a vertical relationship between producers and sellers. The literature on trade policy ignores one important aspect of real life, viz., the fact that often producers and sellers of a commodity are different entities. For example, Toyota cars are sold abroad by dealers that are nationals of the country where the cars are sold. Another example is the clothing industry where items are usually sold by big stores under their own brand names (e.g., St. Michael for Marks and Spencer) but often produced not by the stores but by other domestic and/or foreign producers. Therefore, in deciding an optimal tariff on a commodity, clearly one has to take into account its effect on the domestic seller's profits. In chapter 5 the distinction between producers and sellers is explicitly treated. A number of alternative market structures are considered. It is found that the sign of the optimal tariff may depend on the nature of the producer–seller relationship, viz., who the leader is. In particular, we find that the optimal tariff is negative when the only seller is the leader and there is only one foreign producer. There is also a case where it is optimal for the government of the home country to subsidize imports no matter who the leader is.

Chapter 6 on the other hand considers the FDI aspect of chapter 3. Since one of the main reasons for attracting FDI is to promote employment in the host countries, this chapter assumes the existence of unemployment by incorporating wage income explicitly in the welfare function.

Chapters 7–10 extend the model of chapter 6 in different directions. However, the common thread in these extensions is the endogeneity of FDI. Whereas in chapter 6 the magnitude of FDI is treated in an exogenous manner and is directly controlled by the host government, in chapters 7–10 we assume that the host country is small in the market for FDI and that there is free entry and exit of foreign firms. Thus the number of foreign firms located in the host country is endogenous. It needs to be pointed out that our treatment of FDI is rather novel and significantly different from the traditional treatment in which one considers *one* firm's choice between investing in *one* host country or exporting to that country. Although this traditional treatment made a lot of sense when the extent of FDI was rather limited, in today's world, where FDI is pervasive, a new approach is called for. It is not only because the number of countries that actively welcome FDI is numerous, but also because the number of firms that take part in FDI is very large.

In order to address the new reality in FDI, we introduce a concept of *small open economy in FDI* which faces an exogenous reservation profit rate for investors. Foreign firms enter and exit this small open economy until the profit rate equals the reservation level. The 'outside option' for a foreign firm taking part in FDI is not to export but to locate in one of many other locations.

Within this overall approach that we follow in chapters 7–10, in chapter 7 FDI takes place for a non-tradeable commodity, and the number of domestic firms is exogenous. The host country uses two instruments, viz., profit taxation and a local content requirement (LCR), to compete for FDI in the international market. The foreign firms, in the absence of any restriction, would buy all their inputs from the home country. However, the host country imposes restrictions on the input use of the foreign firms. In particular, it specifies that a certain minimum proportion of the inputs should be bought from the host country. This promotes domestic employment and the profits of domestic firms, but reduces consumers' surplus via a reduction in the amount of foreign supply. It also reduces the number of foreign firms (and thus employment by them) by decreasing their profits. By taking into account all these effects we establish the structure of optimal policies and their relationship to the number, and the relative efficiency levels, of the domestic firms.

In chapter 8 FDI is completely export oriented in the sense that the commodity produced with FDI is fully exported to another country where there is a domestic firm. The host country earns surplus only by setting an LCR so that FDI uses local labour to some extent. FDI in one of the countries within an economic union often creates tensions between the host country and another member country which is a target of exports. For example, Nissan's investment in the United Kingdom created tensions between the United Kingdom and France in the late 1980s because France refused to accept Nissan cars as 'European' to protect French automobile producers. Chapter 8 develops a model which can examine such tensions. In particular, we analyse the conflict between the two countries in the specification of the level of local content of inputs for the foreign firms. We find situations where the host country would want a less severe restriction on local contents than the other country, and vice versa. We consider two cases depending on whether or not the foreign firms have the outside options of investment.

Lobbying by domestic interest groups plays an important role in a government's policy-making decisions. Chapter 9 focuses on lobbying by trade unions in the determination of an LCR on foreign firms. Workers welcome FDI since it can generate employment. Without local content requirements, however, foreign firms may use only foreign parts and therefore reduce demand for domestic workers. Thus there is an incentive for workers to lobby the government to impose a local content requirement, which in turn harms consumers since it raises the price of the commodity. Furthermore, since stricter local content requirements may drive FDI out of the country, it may not be in the interest of the workers to lobby for the strictest control. We examine the properties of the level of the restriction on input contents that satisfies the political equilibrium.

One of the deficiencies in the analysis in chapter 7 is that we assume the number of domestic firms to be exogenously given but the number of foreign firms to be endogenous. This assumption was made because under free entry and exit of the two heterogeneous groups of firms in an oligopolistic market for a homogeneous good, only the more efficient group will exist in the equilibrium and the less efficient group will be driven out of the market. Chapter 10 extends the model of chapter 7 by endogenising the number of domestic firms and assuming that the foreign and the domestic firms produce differentiated commodities. This chapter thus allows us to analyse the phenomenon of cross-hauling, i.e., the simultaneous inflow of foreign firms and outflow of domestic firms. The instrument used here is not an LCR but lump-sum subsidies to the two groups of firms. Therefore chapter 10 is not only different in terms of the model structure but also analyses an instrument which is widely used in practice to attract FDI. For example, subsidizing a site for the setting up of FDI is commonplace. We analyse the effect of discriminatory and uniform subsidies on the inflow/outflow of domestic and foreign firms and on employment. We also derive some properties of optimal subsidies.

1   Cost asymmetry and industrial policy in a closed economy

1.1   Introduction

Oligopolistic firms restrict their production and earn excess profits. Since an increase in competition is considered to raise each oligopolist's production and make it closer to the first-best level, it is commonly believed that increasing competition among firms raises national welfare. With this theoretical underpinning, antitrust policies are generally designed so that new entries are encouraged and entry barriers are strictly prohibited.

Recently, however, it has been found in the theoretical literature on industrial organization that more competition may well reduce welfare in various contexts. For example, Spence (1984), Stiglitz (1981) and Tandon (1984), while analysing R&D decisions under oligopolistic situations, have pointed out the possibility of welfare loss caused by the existence of potential entrants or by free-entry of identical rival firms. Schmalensee (1976), Suzumura and Kiyono (1987) and von Weizsäcker (1980a, b) found that in a Cournot oligopolistic sector the optimal number of (identical) firms may well be smaller than the equilibrium number of firms with free entry and exit.[1] In these models, the existence of fixed costs (or increasing returns to scale) plays a crucial role in deriving diseconomies of competition. While a new entry raises consumers' surplus, it requires an additional fixed cost. It is shown that the latter cost may well exceed the former benefits.

In this chapter we focus on an asymmetric oligopolistic industry with a fixed number of firms. An uneven technical level amongst firms provides the key ingredient. In the presence of marginal cost differential among firms, less efficient firms have lower market shares than the others. Thus, elimination of a minor firm raises the average efficiency of production in the industry, though at the same time it creates a more oligopolistic market structure that causes total output to decrease and thus consumers' surplus

---

[1] For a more recent analysis of entry–exit policy, see, for example, Agarwal and Barua, 1994; Asplund and Sandin, 1999; Hamilton and Stiegert, 2000.

to decline. This chapter shows that such an improvement in production efficiency may well exceed the welfare loss caused by a more oligopolistic market structure.

The mechanism is rather related to the effect of licensing in Katz and Shapiro (1985), in which they find that, under Cournot oligopoly, a firm's licensing to the other may well reduce total surplus. In order to highlight the difference in mechanism, we ignore the existence of fixed costs. In this setting the perverse beneficial effect of elimination of a firm presented by Schmalensee and others disappears, and yet elimination of a minor firm is shown to increase national welfare.

The basic model is spelt out in section 1.2. Section 1.3 then derives the welfare effect of a cost reduction in a firm, or elimination of it, under general demand and cost functions. It derives critical values of market shares of a firm below which helping the firm reduces national welfare or elimination of it maximizes national welfare. In section 1.4, we consider linear demand and cost functions and obtain numerical values of these critical shares for different values for the number of firms in the industry. Section 1.5 considers a tax-cum-subsidy policy (financed through lump-sum taxation) and derives a critical share of a firm below which subsidizing it reduces national welfare. Finally, in section 1.6 we draw some conclusions.

1.2   The model

Suppose there are n firms producing a homogeneous commodity. We assume constant returns to scale throughout and perfect factor markets so that the marginal (or average) cost of each firm – c_j for firm j – is constant.[2] The technical level of a firm may however differ from that of another firm, i.e., typically $c_i \neq c_j$ for $i \neq j$. Firm j maximizes profits given by

$$\pi_j = [f(D) - c_j]x_j \tag{1.1}$$

à la Cournot, where x_j is firm j's output, D is the total output or demand satisfying $D = \sum x_j$, and $f(\cdot)$ is the inverse demand function, i.e., $p = f(D)$, where p is the price of the commodity. The optimal behaviour of

---

[2] The model can be viewed as a part of a general equilibrium framework in which there is another competitive sector and one factor of production which is perfectly mobile within a country between the two sectors. The competitive sector, which produces the numeraire good, ties down the factor price. Therefore, as far as the oligopolistic sector is concerned, the marginal costs can be taken as given. Moreover, if one assumes the utility function to take a particular (quasi-linear) form as in Krugman (1979), the demand function would be independent of income as it is here.

firm j satisfies

$$\frac{\partial \pi_j}{\partial x_j} = f'(D)x_j + f(D) - c_j = \text{MR}^j - c_j = 0 \tag{1.2}$$

for $j = 1, \ldots n$.

We make two standard assumptions:

$$f' < 0 \quad \text{and} \quad \text{MR}_x^j \, (= f''x_j + f') < 0. \tag{1.3}$$

The first inequality simply means a negatively sloped demand function. The second is a conventional stability condition for Cournot oligopoly (see, for example, assumption (A2) in Hahn 1962).

National welfare W is given by the sum of producers' and consumers' surplus, i.e., $W = \sum_{j=1}^{n} \pi_j + \text{CS}$. It is well known that consumers' surplus CS satisfies $d\text{CS} = -Ddp$ so that

$$dW = d\left(\sum_{j=1}^{n} \pi_j\right) - Ddp. \tag{1.4}$$

Using the above model, in the following section we analyse the effect of technical progress – or, equivalently a reduction in the marginal cost – of a firm on national welfare. Without loss of generality, we deal with the effect of changes in firm 1's marginal cost c_1 on welfare.

1.3   Cost reduction and national welfare

Using the model developed in section 1.2 we examine the effect of a firm's cost reduction on national welfare. It will be shown that a minor firm's cost reduction reduces welfare.

Differentiating (1.1) and (1.2) totally and then substituting the relevant terms in (1.4) yield

$$(-\Delta) \cdot \frac{dW}{dc_1} = -x_1 \left\{ 2\left(f' + \sum_{j \neq 1} \text{MR}_x^j\right) + \text{MR}_x^1 \right\} + \sum_{j \neq 1} x_j \text{MR}_x^j \tag{1.5}$$

where

$$\Delta = f' + \sum_{j=1}^{n} \text{MR}_x^j < 0. \tag{1.6}$$

The first term on the right-hand side of (1.5) is negative whereas the second term is positive. Therefore, a cost reduction in firm 1 has two opposing effects on welfare. These two effects can be explained as follows. First, a reduction in c_1 results in an increase in total output, which clearly

W

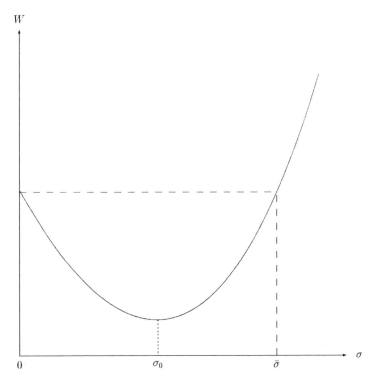

Figure 1.1   Critical shares for a minor firm

benefits the economy. The other effect is a change in profits for all the firms. If firm 1 has lower profits than the others, a decrease in c_1 results in a small rise in profits for this firm, which may be dominated by a large drop in profits for the other firms. In other words, the cost-reducing technical progress in a less efficient firm, which has a minor share of the market, shifts production from the more efficient firms to the less efficient one. Consequently, producers' surplus may fall. The two terms on the right-hand side of (1.5) precisely represent the above two opposing effects. If the beneficial effect on consumers' surplus is dominated by the harmful effect on producers' surplus, a cost reduction in a minor firm will decrease national welfare even though we ignore R&D costs.[3] It may be noteworthy that fixed costs have nothing to do with this result.

From equation (1.5), one can directly derive the following properties. First, if the firms are identical, i.e., $c_i = c_j$ and therefore $x_i = x_j = D/n$

[3] R&D costs will be explicitly considered in chapter 2.

for all i and j, equation (1.5) reduces to

$$\frac{dW}{dc_1} = -\frac{D\left(2f' + \sum_{j=1}^{n} \mathrm{MR}_x^j\right)}{n\Delta} < 0. \tag{1.7}$$

Thus, a cost reduction in any firm always improves national welfare. This is because there cannot be any reallocation of production from more efficient to less efficient firms in this case, as all firms are equally efficient.

Second, if c_i's are such that x_1 is relatively insignificant, the welfare improving effect – the first term in (1.5) – disappears and one is left only with the welfare reducing effect of the cost reduction. On the other hand, if x_1 is relatively large, the first term in (1.5) dominates the second and hence welfare improves. In fact, if $x_1 \geq D/3$, i.e., if firm 1's share of the market is greater than a third, then $x_j < (2/3)D$ for any $j \neq 1$. Since in (1.5) the coefficient of x_1 is negative and that of x_j is positive, substituting $D/3$ for x_1 and $(2/3)D$ for x_j give

$$\frac{dW}{dc_1} < -\frac{D\{2f' + \mathrm{MR}_x^1\}}{3\Delta} < 0 \quad \text{if} \quad x_1 \geq \frac{D}{3}.$$

This implies that in this case a cost reduction in firm 1 increases welfare regardless of the number of rival firms.

Thus we have established the following proposition.

Proposition 1.1 *In Cournot oligopoly a marginal cost reduction in a firm with a sufficiently low market share decreases national welfare, while that for a major firm whose share is higher than $1/3$ increases welfare. If the market share is equally distributed among all firms, a cost reduction in any firm benefits the country.*

Clearly, technical progress in firm 1 increases its market share which is denoted by σ. Thus, from proposition 1.1, national welfare first declines and then rises as firm 1's technical level increases, i.e., there is a 'U' shaped relationship between σ and national welfare, as is illustrated in figure 1.1. One can find two critical values of σ from this relationship. First, σ_0 is the value of σ at which welfare attains the lowest value. Proposition 1.1 is about σ_0. The implication of σ_0 is that if a firm's market share is less than that fraction, helping the firm reduces welfare. Second, $\bar{\sigma}$ is the level of σ at which national welfare has the same level as that at $\sigma = 0$. The implication of this critical value is that if a firm's share is below $\bar{\sigma}$, elimination of the firm improves welfare. Formally,

Proposition 1.2 *In Cournot oligopoly national welfare increases if a firm with a sufficiently low share is removed from the market.*

The two propositions can provide a rationale for some of the industrial policies followed in Japan since the 1950s. Policies favouring major firms and harming minor ones were actually carried out in Japan. MITI (Ministry of International Trade and Industry) selected only major firms and organized R&D groups. Consequently, the members of the groups had better access to innovation than the minor firms. MITI also restricted the number of firms in some industries by urging minor firms to merge or exit under the name of industrial structure adjustment policy.[4]

1.4   A linear example

In the previous section, we pointed out the possibility of a loss of national welfare caused by an increase in a minor firm's market share under general assumptions. In this section, we assume the linearity of the demand curve, and derive some figures for critical shares σ_0 and $\bar{\sigma}$ explained in the previous section. We shall notice that under the linearity assumption, the critical shares are rather high. In other words, technical progress for a firm with a considerably high share may be harmful, and that elimination of such a firm may be beneficial to the country.

If the demand function is given by

$$p = \alpha - \beta D, \tag{1.8}$$

equation (1.5) reduces to

$$\frac{dW}{dc_1} = \frac{\beta[2(n+1)x_1 - D]}{\Delta}. \tag{1.9}$$

Therefore, the critical share $\sigma_0 (= x_1/D)$ is

$$\sigma_0 = \frac{1}{2(n+1)}. \tag{1.10}$$

So long as σ is smaller than σ_0, firm 1's technical progress decreases national welfare. Table 1.1 presents critical share σ_0 for different values of n. For example, in the case of triopoly, so long as the share for a firm is less than 12.5%, its technical progress reduces national welfare. Table 1.1 also gives the average share of the other firms (σ_0'). The difference between the 'minor' firm whose technical progress is harmful and the average of the others becomes very small as the number of firms increases.

We next obtain critical share $\bar{\sigma}$ for firm 1, i.e., eliminating firm 1 benefits the country if it has a lower share than $\bar{\sigma}$. From (1.1), (1.5) and (1.8) we obtain

$$\pi_j = (p - c_j)x_j = \beta x_j^2. \tag{1.11}$$

---

[4] See Komiya, Okuno and Suzumura (1988) for various examples of such policies.

Table 1.1   *Critical shares for welfare-reducing technical change*

n	σ_0 (in %)	σ_0' (in %)
2	16.7	83.3
3	12.5	43.8
4	10.0	30.0
5	8.3	22.9
6	7.1	18.6
7	6.3	15.6
8	5.6	13.5
9	5.0	11.9
10	4.5	10.6

Therefore, under the demand function given in (1.8) the sum of producers' and consumers' surplus is

$$W = \sum_{j=1}^{n} \pi_j - pD + \left(\alpha D - \frac{\beta D^2}{2} \right)$$
$$= \beta \left(\sum_{j=1}^{n} x_j^2 + \frac{D^2}{2} \right). \tag{1.12}$$

Using the above welfare function, we shall now obtain critical share $\bar{\sigma}$.
   Substituting (1.8) into (1.2) yields

$$D = \frac{n\alpha - \sum_{j=1}^{n} c_j}{(n+1)\beta}, \tag{1.13}$$

$$x_j = \frac{\alpha - nc_j + \sum_{k \neq j} c_k}{(n+1)\beta}. \tag{1.14}$$

From (1.12) and (1.14) we find

$$(n+1)^2 \beta W = \left(n + \frac{n^2}{2} \right) \alpha^2 - (n+2)\alpha \cdot \sum_{j=1}^{n} c_j$$
$$- \left(n + \frac{3}{2} \right) \left(\sum_{j=1}^{n} c_j \right)^2 + (n+1)^2 \sum_{j=1}^{n} c_j^2. \tag{1.15}$$

Thus W is represented as a function of c_j's. Let us fix c_k ($k = 2, \ldots, n$) and vary c_1. If for $c_1 = c_1^0$ the value of x_1 given in (1.14) is zero, $W(c_1^0)$ is the welfare level for the case where firm 1 is eliminated. Therefore, if for the actual level of c_1 the welfare level is lower than $W(c_1^0)$, elimination of firm 1 makes the country better off.

Table 1.2 *Critical shares for welfare-improving elimination of a minor firm*

n	$\bar{\sigma}$ (in %)	$\bar{\sigma}'$ (in %)
2	30.8	69.2
3	24.0	38.0
4	19.5	26.8
5	16.4	20.9
6	14.1	17.2
7	12.4	14.6
8	11.0	12.7
9	9.9	11.3
10	9.1	10.1

From (1.14) for firm 1, c_1^0 is given by

$$c_1^0 = \frac{\alpha + \sum_{k \neq 1} c_k}{n}. \tag{1.16}$$

Substituting (1.16) into (1.15), and solving the following equation:

$$W(c_1) = W(c_1^0),$$

we find the critical level of c_1 as

$$\bar{c}_1 = \frac{\left(1 + \frac{1}{2n}\right)\alpha + \left(n + 2 + \frac{1}{2n}\right)\sum_{j \neq 1} c_j}{n^2 + n - \frac{1}{2}}. \tag{1.17}$$

Substituting (1.17) into (1.14) and manipulating them, we obtain $\bar{\sigma}$, the critical share for firm 1 below which eliminating this firm increases national welfare,

$$\bar{\sigma} = \frac{n}{n^2 + n + \frac{1}{2}}, \tag{1.18}$$

which only depends on the number of firms n.

Table 1.2 presents $\bar{\sigma}$ for various values of n. For example, in the case of triopoly, if a firm has a share lower than 24% (say, the distribution is 20%, 35%, 45%) the country can increase national welfare by eliminating the firm. Table 1.2 also shows the average share of the other firms ($\bar{\sigma}'$). It may be noteworthy that the difference between the share of the firm whose elimination benefits the country and the average share of the others is very small especially when the number of firms is large.

1.5   Production tax-cum-subsidy

Let us next consider the effect of a production tax-cum-subsidy on national welfare. We shall derive a similar property to the previous analysis, i.e., a tax on minor firms and a subsidy to major ones are beneficial to the country.

If tax t_j is imposed on production by firm j, the optimal condition for firm j becomes

$$\text{MR}^j = p + f'x_j = c_j + t_j. \tag{1.19}$$

Differentiating (1.19) totally, we derive

$$\text{MR}^j_x dD + f'dx_j = dt_j. \tag{1.20}$$

Adding (1.20) over all j's and using (1.6) yield

$$\Delta dD = \sum_{k=1}^{n} dt_k,$$

$$f'dx_j = dt_j - \frac{\text{MR}^j_x \sum_{k=1}^{n} dt_k}{\Delta}. \tag{1.21}$$

In the presence of production taxes and subsidies, national welfare W equals $\sum_{j=1}^{n} \pi_j + \text{CS} + \sum_{j=1}^{n} t_j x_j$ so that a change in W is given by

$$dW = d\left(\sum_{j=1}^{n} \pi_j\right) - Ddp + d\left(\sum_{j=1}^{n} t_j x_j\right),$$

and thus

$$dW = d\left(\sum_{k=1}^{n} (p - c_k)x_k\right) - Df'dD. \tag{1.22}$$

Substituting (1.21) into (1.22) and rearranging the terms, we have

$$\Delta f'dW = \sum_{k=1}^{n} \left\{ \left(f' + \sum_{j=1}^{n} \text{MR}^j_x\right)(p - c_k) - \sum_{j=1}^{n}(p - c_j)\text{MR}^j_x \right\} dt_k. \tag{1.23}$$

Therefore, from (1.6) and (1.19), we get

$$\left.\frac{dW}{dt_k}\right|_{\forall t_j = 0} = \frac{f'x_k + \sum_{j \neq k} \text{MR}^j_x (x_k - x_j)}{(-\Delta)}. \tag{1.24}$$

From (1.3), (1.6) and (1.24), we find that if x_k is sufficiently small, (1.24) is positive. However, if firm k has the largest share, (1.24) is negative. Furthermore, if $x_j = D/n$ for all the firms, (1.24) becomes negative. Formally,

Table 1.3 *Critical shares for a welfare-reducing production subsidy*

n	$\tilde{\sigma}$ (in %)
2	33.3
3	25.0
4	20.0
5	16.7
6	14.3
7	12.5
8	11.1
9	10.0
10	9.1

Proposition 1.3 *A marginal tax (subsidy) on production by a firm with a sufficiently small (large) share increases national welfare. If the share is equally distributed among all the firms, a marginal subsidy benefits the country.*

In order to find a simple expression for the critical share at which $dW/dt_k = 0$, let us assume the linear demand function given by (1.8). Substituting (1.8) into (1.24), we find

$$\Delta \left. \frac{dW}{dt_k} \right|_{\forall_{t_j=0}} = -\beta(n+1)D\left(\frac{1}{n+1} - \sigma_k\right), \tag{1.25}$$

where $\sigma_k (= x_k/D)$ is the share of firm k. Therefore, critical share $\tilde{\sigma}$ is

$$\tilde{\sigma} = \frac{1}{n+1}, \tag{1.26}$$

whose values are given in table 1.3 for different values of n.

For example, if there are five firms whose shares are 33%, 25%, 19%, 14%, 9%, marginal production subsidies for the first three firms and marginal production taxes on the last two firms increase national welfare. Thus, a tax policy which favours major firms and impairs minor firms may benefit the country even if it seems to reduce competition among firms.

Though it seems striking, it is rather plausible since the policy shifts production from less efficient firms to more efficient ones. In order to see the point, let us consider the first-best tax-cum-subsidy policy. Equation (1.23) shows that a prohibitive tax on all the firms except the most efficient firm and a (Marshallian) subsidy for the most efficient firm that makes the actual marginal cost equal to the price are the best policy. In other words, under the optimal tax-cum-subsidy policy only the most efficient firm should be in operation and produce the Pareto optimal level of output.

1.6   Conclusion

Policies favouring minor firms, such as a production subsidy and an entry promotion policy, cause a more competitive market structure. A minor firm's technical progress not only creates a more competitive market structure but also raises the average efficiency of production. Therefore, these policies and changes are widely believed to benefit the country. Conversely, it may be said that exit of minor firms and policies impairing them strengthen the oligopolistic position of major firms and consequently decrease national welfare. Such a belief forms a backbone for various antitrust policies in many countries across the globe. However, in this chapter we have established that elimination of minor firms and tax-cum-subsidy policies which favour major firms and harm minor ones increase national welfare. Moreover, a minor firm's technical progress reduces national welfare.

These results are based on the following logic. Generally speaking, minor firms have less efficient technology than major ones. Under perfect competition, the most efficient allocation of production is attained. However, under Cournot oligopoly, the allocation of production among firms is not Pareto optimal. Technical progress for a minor firm (or a less efficient firm) increases production by the less efficient firm and decreases production by the more efficient firms. Thus, the allocation of production is further distorted and national welfare may be lowered although the technical progress itself is beneficial. If all the firms are identical, the harmful effect does not appear since a change in allocation of production exercises only a negligible effect. Tax-cum-subsidy policies which favour minor firms and harm major firms exert the same harmful effect as above.

On the other hand, tax-cum-subsidy policies favouring major (more efficient) firms and impairing minor (less efficient) firms, and elimination of minor firms shift production from the less efficient firms to the more efficient ones: they redress the misallocation of production. Consequently, national welfare increases. Thus, some industrial policies carried out by MITI in Japan, such as selection of major firms as members of R&D groups and elimination of minor firms by grouping firms or urging mergers, might be given a rationale.

2   R&D policy

2.1   Introduction

In the previous chapter we considered the effect on national welfare of a minor firm's exogenous technical progress. However, technical progress usually occurs as a result of R&D investment. In this chapter we extend the analysis of chapter 1 by considering endogenous R&D investment by Cournot duopolists with initial cost differentials, and examine the structure of optimum R&D tax-cum-subsidies.

We conduct our analysis by developing a two-stage game of duopoly. In the first stage both firms decide on their cost-reducing R&D investments, and in the second they compete in a quantity-setting game. Much has been written on such two-stage models (see, for example, Bagwell and Staiger, 1994; Besley and Suzumura, 1992; Brander and Spencer, 1983; d'Aspremont and Jacquemin, 1988; Katz, 1986; Okuno-Fujiwara and Suzumura, 1993; Petit and SannaRandaccio, 2000; Rowthorn, 1992; Spence, 1984; Spencer and Brander, 1983; Suzumura, 1992; Varian, 1995). However, most of the authors work with models of symmetric oligopoly. Only Spencer and Brander (1983) consider asymmetry in marginal-cost levels. In their model rival firms which belong to two different countries compete only in a third country and the strategic use of government policies is at the heart of their analysis. They ignore the effect of R&D subsidies on consumers' surplus in the third country, and focus on only the international distribution of profits.

Although the literature on endogenous R&D is fairly large, very few authors analyse the question of R&D subsidies. The papers that deal with R&D subsidies (such as Spencer and Brander 1983 and Spence 1984) do not allow for the effect of such subsidies on the distribution of profits among domestic firms. For example, Spence (1984) assumes a demand function with constant elasticity (for which the demand function is convex) and symmetric oligopoly, and finds that the optimal R&D subsidy rate is positive. We generalize this result by considering a general demand function, and find that the optimal R&D subsidy rate is positive if the demand function is convex but negative if it is concave.

Spencer and Brander (1983), on the other hand, emphasize the profit-shifting effect of R&D subsidies in the context of international rivalry. In this chapter using a closed economy model it will be shown that the distribution of profits among *domestic firms* has a very important implication for national welfare. For example, allowing for asymmetry in the marginal-cost level among duopolists, we find that the firm with a higher market share should be subsidized in its R&D activities and the other taxed so as to maximize national welfare. The distribution of profits among the firms with different initial costs is a key factor behind our results.

The layout of this chapter is as follows. The model is set up in section 2.2. A number of comparative static exercises are carried out in section 2.3. In section 2.4 we examine the welfare effect of helping a minor firm and see how the existence of R&D investments affects the critical share obtained in the previous chapter. The properties of optimal R&D subsidies are derived in section 2.5, in two subsections. Whereas subsection 2.5.1 considers uniform subsidies under symmetric duopoly, subsection 2.5.2 characterizes optimal discriminatory subsidies under asymmetric oligopoly. Finally, section 2.6 concludes.

2.2   The model

We consider a market in which there are two firms (1 and 2) with different initial marginal costs. They compete in a two-stage game. In stage 1 each firm invests in R&D, which determines the level of the marginal cost in stage 2. In stage 2 the firms compete with each other for the determination of outputs, taking R&D levels as given in the previous stage. The firms are assumed to play Cournot-Nash games in both stages, and we consider the subgame perfect equilibrium of the two-stage game.

The marginal cost of firm i, c_i, is given by

$$c_i = k_i + g(h_i), \ g' < 0, \tag{2.1}$$

where k_i represents firm i's primary marginal cost which does not depend on R&D investment, and h_i represents firm i's R&D investment. Primary-cost differentials may be due to some firm-specific knowledge or access to special resources, such as locations, raw materials and imported technologies, which may be caused by discriminatory regulations. It is to be noted that we consider only a special case of a more general specification of the costs given by $c_i = H_i(k_i, h_i)$.

Profits π_i and net cash flow v_i of firm i are

$$\pi_i = (f(D) - c_i)x_i, \tag{2.2}$$

$$v_i = \pi_i - (1 - s_i)h_i, \tag{2.3}$$

where $f(D)$ is the inverse demand function, i.e., $p = f(D)$, where p is the price of the commodity, and x_i and s_i are the output levels and the R&D subsidy rate respectively for firm i. D is the aggregate output, i.e.,

$$D = x_1 + x_2. \tag{2.4}$$

The profit maximizing conditions in the output game are

$$c_i = f'(D)x_i + f(D) \implies x_i = x_i(c_1, c_2). \tag{2.5}$$

We assume the inverse demand function to satisfy

Assumption 2.1

$$f'(D) < 0 \quad and \quad f'(D) + f''(D)x_i < 0 \quad for\ all \quad 0 \le x_i \le D.$$

The first property of assumption 2.1 implies a negatively sloped demand curve, and the second property corresponds to the 'normal' case in Seade (1980, pp. 483–4) and also to strategic substitutes in Bulow, Geanakoplos and Klemperer (1985) and Dixit (1986). This also guarantees the concavity of each firm's profit function. Totally differentiating equation (2.5) for both firms and using assumption 2.1, we get

$$\frac{\partial x_i}{\partial c_i} = \frac{f''x_j + 2f'}{f'(f''D + 3f')} < 0, \quad \frac{\partial x_i}{\partial c_j} = -\frac{f''x_i + f'}{f'(f''D + 3f')} > 0$$

$$\text{and} \quad \frac{\partial D}{\partial c_i} = \frac{1}{f''D + 3f'} < 0. \tag{2.6}$$

In the R&D game, firm i maximizes v_i defined by (2.3) with respect to h_i, given the other firm's R&D investment (and hence c_j, $j \ne i$). Using (2.5) we derive the first order conditions for this problem as

$$\left. \frac{dv_i}{dh_i} \right|_{h_j = \text{constant}} = \left[f'(D(c_1, c_2)) \frac{\partial x_j(c_1, c_2)}{\partial c_i} - 1 \right] x_i(c_1, c_2) g'(h_i) - (1 - s_i)$$

$$\equiv \psi^i(h_1, h_2, k_1, k_2, s_i) = 0. \tag{2.7}$$

National welfare W is

$$W = v_1 + v_2 + \text{CS} - s_1 h_1 - s_2 h_2, \tag{2.8}$$

where CS represents consumers' surplus. It is well known that

$$d\text{CS} = -Ddp. \tag{2.9}$$

Totally differentiating equations (2.1)–(2.5), (2.7) and (2.8) and using (2.9) we find

$$
\begin{aligned}
dW = {}& -f'(x_1 dx_1 + x_2 dx_2) - x_1 dc_1 - x_2 dc_2 - dh_1 - dh_2 \\
= {}& \left[-f'g'(h_1) \left(x_1 \frac{\partial D}{\partial c_1} + x_2 \frac{\partial x_2}{\partial c_1} \right) - s_1 \right] dh_1 \\
& + \left[-f'g'(h_2) \left(x_2 \frac{\partial D}{\partial c_2} + x_1 \frac{\partial x_1}{\partial c_2} \right) - s_2 \right] dh_2 \\
& - \left[\frac{x_1(f''x_2 + 2f') - y_2(f''x_2 + f') + x_1(f''D + 3f')}{f''D + 3f'} \right] dk_1 \\
& - \left[\frac{x_2(f''x_1 + 2f') - x_1(f''x_1 + f') + x_2(f''D + 3f')}{f''D + 3f'} \right] dk_2,
\end{aligned}
$$

$$(2.10)$$

where $\partial D/\partial c_i$ and $\partial x_i/\partial c_j$ are given in (2.6). The above equation forms the backbone of our subsequent welfare analysis.

2.3   Comparative statics

In this section we derive a few results on the comparative statics of our model which will be used for the welfare analyses of sections 2.4 and 2.5. In particular, we obtain the effects of changes in primary marginal costs and R&D subsidies on the equilibrium values of R&D investments.

Totally differentiating (2.7) for $i = 1$ and 2 we obtain[1]

$$\psi_1^1 dh_1 + \psi_2^1 dh_2 + \psi_3^1 dk_1 + \psi_4^1 dk_2 + ds_1 = 0, \qquad (2.11)$$

$$\psi_1^2 dh_1 + \psi_2^2 dh_2 + \psi_3^2 dk_1 + \psi_4^2 dk_2 + ds_2 = 0. \qquad (2.12)$$

We assume the stability of the present Cournot duopoly and the concavity of the value functions.[2] That is,

Assumption 2.2

$$\psi_1^1 < 0, \quad \psi_2^2 < 0, \quad and \ \Delta_3 \equiv \psi_1^1 \psi_2^2 - \psi_2^1 \psi_1^2 > 0.$$

Furthermore, an increase in the primary marginal cost reduces the potential profitability of the firm and hence it is assumed to decrease the marginal contribution of R&D investment. Since an increase in the

[1] ψ_j^i is the partial derivative of $\psi^i(\cdot)$ with respect to the jth argument.

[2] Assumption 2.1 guarantees the uniqueness of a solution in the output game, and assumption 2.2 that of a solution in the first stage of the game.

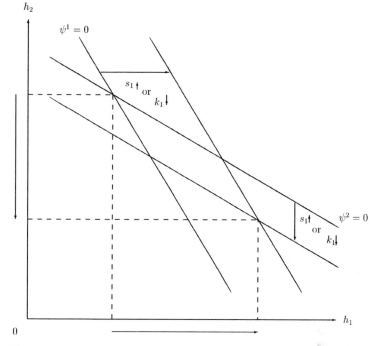

Figure 2.1 Comparative statics

primary marginal cost also increases the potential profitability of the rival firm, we assume that it raises the marginal contribution of the rival firm's R&D investment.[3] These properties are summarised as

Assumption 2.3

$$\psi_3^1 < 0, \ \psi_4^2 < 0, \ \psi_4^1 \left(= \frac{\psi_2^1}{g'(h_2)} \right) > 0, \ \text{and} \ \psi_3^2 \left(= \frac{\psi_1^2}{g'(h_1)} \right) > 0.$$

Since from (2.1) the third and fourth inequalities above imply that $\psi_2^1 < 0$ and $\psi_1^2 < 0$, it follows from assumption 2.2, equations (2.11) and (2.12) that the two firms are strategic substitutes in the R&D game. Figure 2.1 illustrates the reaction functions in this R&D game, ψ^1 and ψ^2 being defined in (2.7).

Under assumptions 2.2 and 2.3 the following property with respect to the level of each firm's R&D investment is obtained.

---

[3] It can be verified that both these properties hold for the case of, for example, linear demand functions.

Proposition 2.1 *A firm with a lower (higher) primary marginal cost invests more (less) in R&D.*

Proof. From (2.11) and (2.12),

$$\frac{dh_1}{dk_1} = \frac{-\psi_3^1\psi_2^2 + \psi_3^2\psi_2^1}{\Delta_3} \quad \text{and} \quad \frac{dh_2}{dk_1} = \frac{-\psi_1^1\psi_3^2 + \psi_1^2\psi_3^1}{\Delta_3},$$

whence, using assumptions 2.2 and 2.3, it follows that

$$\frac{dh_1}{dk_1} < 0, \quad \frac{dh_2}{dk_1} > 0. \tag{2.13}$$

Since $h_1 = h_2$ when the two firms are fully symmetric, this equation shows that a firm with even a slight advantage in the primary marginal cost invests more in R&D.   □

The property of proposition 2.1 is illustrated in figure 2.1. Since a decrease in k_1 shifts the ψ^1 curve rightward and the ψ^2 curve downward, firm 1's R&D investment rises whereas firm 2's investment declines.

Similarly, using (2.11) and (2.12) we also obtain the comparative statics with respect to the R&D subsidy rates. Under assumptions 2.2 and 2.3 these are

$$\frac{dh_i}{ds_j} = \frac{\psi_j^i}{\Delta_3} < 0, \quad \text{and} \quad \frac{dh_i}{ds_i} = -\frac{\psi_j^j}{\Delta_3} > 0, \quad i \neq j. \tag{2.14}$$

As one would expect, an R&D subsidy to a firm stimulates its own R&D investment and reduces that of the other.

The effect of an increase in s_1 on the two firms' R&D investment is also illustrated in figure 2.1. It shifts the ψ^1 curve rightward and the ψ^2 curve downward, and hence firm 1's R&D investment increases whereas firm 2's investment declines.

2.4   Cost reduction and national welfare

This section ignores R&D subsidies and examines the welfare effect of a change in firm 1's primary marginal cost (k_1), which affects its market share, and thereby investigates the relationship between the market share and welfare. To be more specific, taking $s_1 = s_2 = 0$ and k_2 as fixed, we compare the welfare-minimizing value of k_1 in the presence of R&D investment analysed in this chapter with that in the absence of R&D investment considered in chapter 1. As shown in chapter 1, this analysis gives us a value of the market share of firm 1 such that if the actual market share of firm 1 is below this critical share, then any technical progress in firm 1 makes the country worse off. We shall show below that for traditional forms of demand functions (such as linear or constant-elasticity demand functions), this critical share is higher in the presence of R&D investment than in the absence of it.

Let k_1^0 be the value of k_1 that minimises welfare (W) when the levels of R&D investments are kept constant at their equilibrium levels. In this case dW/dc_1 as given by (1.5) in chapter 1 is zero. Thus, from (2.10) we obtain

$$\left.\frac{dW}{dk_1}\right|_{k_1=k_1^0} = \left[-f'g'(h_1)\left(x_1\frac{\partial D}{\partial c_1} + x_2\frac{\partial x_2}{\partial c_1}\right)\right]\frac{dh_1}{dk_1}$$
$$+ \left[-f'g'(h_2)\left(x_2\frac{\partial D}{\partial c_2} + x_1\frac{\partial x_1}{\partial c_2}\right)\right]\frac{dh_2}{dk_1}. \qquad (2.15)$$

Substituting (2.6) into (2.15) yields

$$\{3f' + f''D\}\left.\frac{dW}{dk_1}\right|_{k_1=k_1^0} = \{(f''x_2+f')x_2-f'x_1\}\left(g'(h_1)\frac{dh_1}{dk_1} - g'(h_2)\frac{dh_2}{dk_1}\right)$$
$$+ \left(x_1^2 + x_2^2\right)f''g'(h_2)\frac{dh_2}{dk_1}. \qquad (2.16)$$

When dW/dc_1 given by (1.5) in chapter 1 is zero (which holds when $k_1 = k_1^0$), because of assumption 2.1 we have

$$(f''x_2 + f')x_2 - f'x_1 = x_1((2f' + f''D) + (2f' + f''x_2)) < 0.$$

Therefore, from (2.1), (2.13) and (2.16), we get

$$\left.\frac{dW}{dk_1}\right|_{k_1=k_1^0} > 0 \quad \text{if} \quad f'' \geq 0.$$

It therefore follows that when $f'' > 0$ the welfare-minimizing value of k_1 in the presence of R&D is less than k_1^0, and thus the critical market share of firm 1 is higher in the presence of R&D than that in the absence of R&D. In figure 2.2, $\tilde{\sigma}_0$ is the market share of firm 1 when k_1 is at the welfare minimizing level. As can be seen from figure 2.2, $\tilde{\sigma}_0$ is greater than σ_0 which is the critical market share for firm 1 in the absence of any R&D.

To summarize, when $f'' > 0$, the endogeneity of R&D makes the case of helping a minor firm even weaker. This is because a primary cost reduction for the minor firm has an additional cost-reducing effect via an increase in R&D investment. This helps the minor firm to capture a bigger share of the market at the expense of the more efficient firm. Therefore, the reduction in the overall efficiency is more when R&D exists than when it is absent.

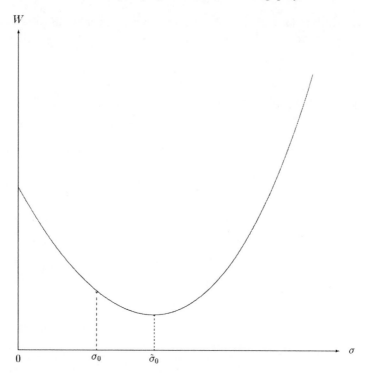

Figure 2.2 Critical shares in the presence and absence of R&D

2.5   R&D subsidy and welfare

We next examine the welfare effects of R&D subsidies and obtain the optimal R&D subsidies.

2.5.1   The case of symmetric duopoly

First we deal with the case of symmetric duopoly where $k_1 = k_2$ and $s_1 = s_2 = s$. Substituting (2.6) into (2.10), we find the welfare effect of R&D subsidies:

$$\left(\frac{dW}{ds_1} + \frac{dW}{ds_2}\right)_{s_1=s_2=s} = 2\left(\frac{f''x_1^2 g'}{(f''D + 3f')} - s\right)\left(\frac{dh_1}{ds_1} + \frac{dh_1}{ds_2}\right),$$

(2.17)

where from (2.14) we have

$$\frac{dh_1}{ds_1} + \frac{dh_1}{ds_2} = -\frac{\left(\psi_2^2 - \psi_2^1\right)}{\Delta_3}.$$

Since $\psi_1^1 = \psi_2^2$ and $\psi_2^1 = \psi_1^2$ in the symmetric case, using the definition of Δ_3 given in assumption 2.2, we get

$$\left(\psi_2^2 - \psi_2^1\right)_{s_1=s_2=s \ \& \ k_1=k_2} = \frac{\Delta_3}{\psi_1^1 + \psi_1^2}.$$

From the above two equations and assumptions 2.2 and 2.3 it follows that

$$\left(\frac{dh_1}{ds_1} + \frac{dh_1}{ds_2}\right)_{s_1=s_2=s \ \& \ k_1=k_2} = -\frac{1}{\psi_1^1 + \psi_1^2} > 0.$$

By substituting the above equation into (2.17) and using (2.1) and assumption 2.1, we directly obtain the following proposition:

Proposition 2.2 *For the case of symmetric duopoly, the optimal R&D policy is to tax (subsidize) both firms if $f'' < 0$ ($f'' > 0$).[4] When the demand function is linear ($f'' = 0$), no intervention is the optimal R&D policy.*

When the firms determine the levels of R&D investments, they consider the following two aspects. On one hand, because of oligopolistic behaviour firms under-produce and therefore under-invest in R&D. On the other hand, due to strategic interdependence a firm invests more in order to get a higher market share. Thus, whether over-investment or under-investment takes place depends on the magnitude of these two opposing forces.

In the case of linear demand, the two opposing effects cancel each other out and the government does not intervene. However, in the case where $f'' > 0$ ($f'' < 0$) a price reduction caused by a reduction of the marginal cost due to R&D investment increases consumers' surplus more (less) than in the case of linear demand. However, the firms do not take account of consumers' surplus when determining the level of R&D investment. Therefore, the government which is concerned with social welfare attempts to raise (lower) R&D investment by subsidising (taxing) it when $f'' > 0$ ($f'' < 0$).

2.5.2 Optimal discriminatory R&D subsidies

In this subsection we consider the case of asymmetric oligopoly and obtain optimal discriminatory R&D policies.

---

[4] Since Spence (1984) assumes a constant-elasticity demand function (for which $f'' > 0$), the optimal subsidy is positive, as stated here.

From (2.10) the optimal s_1 and s_2 satisfy

$$\frac{dW}{ds_1}\bigg|_{s_2=\text{constant}} = \left[-f'g'(h_1)\left(x_1\frac{\partial D}{\partial c_1} + x_2\frac{\partial x_2}{\partial c_1}\right) - s_1\right]\frac{dh_1}{ds_1}$$
$$+ \left[-f'g'(h_2)\left(x_2\frac{\partial D}{\partial c_2} + x_1\frac{\partial x_1}{\partial c_2}\right) - s_2\right]\frac{dh_2}{ds_1} = 0,$$

(2.18)

$$\frac{dW}{ds_2}\bigg|_{s_1=\text{constant}} = \left[-f'g'(h_1)\left(x_1\frac{\partial D}{\partial c_1} + x_2\frac{\partial x_2}{\partial c_1}\right) - s_1\right]\frac{dh_1}{ds_2}$$
$$+ \left[-f'g'(h_2)\left(x_2\frac{\partial D}{\partial c_2} + x_1\frac{\partial x_1}{\partial c_2}\right) - s_2\right]\frac{dh_2}{ds_2} = 0.$$

(2.19)

Substituting the value of s_1 which satisfies (2.18) into (2.19) we obtain

$$\frac{dW}{ds_2} = (\alpha - s_2)\beta,$$

(2.20)

where

$$\alpha = -f'g'(h_2)\left(x_2\frac{\partial D}{\partial c_2} + x_1\frac{\partial x_1}{\partial c_2}\right),$$

$$\beta = \frac{dh_2}{ds_2} - \frac{dh_1}{ds_2}\left(\frac{dh_2}{ds_1}\bigg/\frac{dh_1}{ds_1}\right).$$

It is to be reiterated that in deriving (2.20) s_1 is not held constant; rather we allow s_1 to vary in a way that it takes the optimal value for every value of s_2. From (2.6), (2.14) and assumption 2.2, α and β are rewritten as

$$\alpha = \frac{-f'g'(h_2)(x_2 - x_1 - (x_1)^2 f''/f')}{f''D + 3f'},$$

$$\beta = -\frac{1}{\psi_2^2} > 0.$$

(2.21)

Using (2.20), (2.21) and assumption 2.1, we derive the following proposition:

Proposition 2.3 *If the market share of the minor firm is sufficiently low, the optimal R&D policy is to subsidize the major and tax the minor firm. In the case of linear demand, even under a slight difference in market shares the optimal R&D policy is to tax the smaller and subsidize the bigger firm.*

Proof. Assuming concavity of the welfare function,[5] and by substituting α in (2.21) into (2.20) and using (2.1) and assumption 2.1, we obtain

$$x_1 \simeq 0 \quad \Rightarrow \quad s_2^* > 0,$$
$$x_2 \simeq 0 \quad \Rightarrow \quad s_2^* < 0.$$

The first property implies that if a firm has a sufficiently small share, the R&D of the other firm should be subsidized. The second property shows that the R&D of a firm with a sufficiently low share should be taxed. Therefore the first half of this proposition is valid.

In the case of linear demand ($f'' = 0$), α in (2.21) satisfies

$$\alpha \gtreqless 0 \quad \text{if and only if} \quad x_1 \lesseqgtr x_2.$$

Therefore, the second half of the proposition follows directly from (2.20).   □

Intuitively, helping a firm by subsidizing its R&D activities increases its profits, decreases the profits of its rival firm and increases consumers' surplus. When the firm that is helped is substantially larger than the other, the increase in its profits dominates all the other benefits and thus raises total surplus. The optimal R&D tax-cum-subsidy policy is therefore to make the most of the superiority of the major firm.

Using the model of asymmetric oligopoly without R&D investment in chapter 1 we showed that removing a firm which contributes little to domestic total surplus is welfare improving. In the presence of R&D investment this property is amplified. Under linear demand, for example, a firm with even a slight cost advantage should be subsidized and the other firm taxed. As is clear from the above analysis, the effect of R&D subsidies on the distribution of profits among domestic firms is a very important factor in the determination of the optimal R&D policy.

2.6   Conclusion

Using an asymmetric Cournot duopoly model with endogenous R&D investment, we first find that a firm with some initial cost advantage invests more in R&D, and consequently the difference in market shares between the two firms extends more as a result of R&D investment. We find that the case for helping a minor firm is weaker in the presence of R&D investment than in the absence of it.

---

[5] It can be easily verified that the welfare function is indeed concave in s_2 under, for example, linear demand. Note that in this welfare function s_1 varies so that it takes the optimal value for each s_2, as mentioned before.

Next, for the case of symmetric duopoly, we find that the shape of the demand function critically affects the sign of the optimum R&D subsidy. In particular, if the demand function is linear, no intervention is the best policy. We also demonstrate that the optimal structure of R&D tax-cum-subsidy policy is to tax the minor firm and to subsidize the major one. Especially in the case of linear demand, even a slight difference in the market share provides a rationale for a discriminatory tax-cum-subsidy policy. Thus, simple applications of antitrust policies may be counter-beneficial in oligopolistic situations.

3 Trade and industrial policy under foreign penetration

3.1 Introduction

We have so far considered a closed economy where domestic oligopolists with different marginal costs compete with each other. This chapter extends this analysis to an open economy context in which foreign firms enter the domestic market and compete with domestic oligopolists.

In the case of a closed economy, helping a minor firm reallocates production from the more efficient firms to the minor firm. If the minor firm is very inefficient and hence its surplus per unit of output is much smaller than that of the other firms, the reallocation of production reduces total producers' surplus so much that this reduction dominates an increase in consumers' surplus, causing total surplus to decline. In the case of foreign direct investment, foreign firms repatriate all their profits to their home country. Thus, from the host country's viewpoint, they are firms that make no contribution to domestic producers' surplus even though they may hold a significant share of the market. Thus, one can expect that helping foreign firms to penetrate may well make the host country worse off. This chapter is devoted to the analysis of this property.

Foreign penetration through direct investment has been a significant issue for a long time in many countries. Direct penetration by big US companies to Europe in various industries since the 1930s aroused widespread fears in European countries, as described in detail by Tugendhat (1971). It has now become a widespread phenomenon all over the world, and the cause of serious international problems.[1] For example, it has been a major economic issue between the United States and Japan. The US has been negotiating with Japan for the opening of various markets, such as construction, banking, and telecommunication to US firms, while more and more Japanese automobile and electric manufacturers have been establishing subsidiaries in the US.

---

[1] See Bergsten, Horst and Moran (1978), Hood and Young (1979, ch. 1) and Vernon (1971).

Foreign penetration by direct investment is often taken to be a danger to host countries, especially from the viewpoint of political economy. It is often claimed that with significant capital from abroad, the control of the national economy shifts to foreign firms, and that the host country is confined only to lower levels of activity and income.[2] On the other hand, the standard economic theory generally points to a beneficial consequence of foreign penetration under the assumption of perfect competition. It shows that improvements in consumers' surplus caused by increases in supply by foreign firms dominate reductions in domestic producers' surplus.[3]

However, it is not necessarily the case that the domestic market structure is competitive. Rather, in most cases, foreign firms penetrate a domestic oligopolistic industry where domestic firms earn high profits restricting entry by other potential domestic firms by exploiting their advantages of technology, better access to resources, etc.[4] Since the high profits are reduced by foreign direct penetration, the harmful effect on producers' surplus is greater in the presence of oligopolistic distortions than under perfect competition, and it might even dominate the beneficial effect on consumers' surplus. Thus, foreign direct penetration in oligopolistic circumstances might be harmful to the host country.

Furthermore, the cost of accepting foreign direct penetration may be so large that even world welfare may decrease. It occurs especially when the foreign firm is not sufficiently efficient. This property is a simple application of the result of chapter 1. Thus, one can say that even if the host country compensates the foreign firm for the loss caused by the restriction, the restriction can benefit the host country.

The effect on national welfare of indirect foreign capital inflows under imperfect competition has been analysed by, among others, Helpman and Razin (1983). They treat inflows of foreign capital as a perfect substitute for domestic capital, viz., indirect capital movements. Instead of indirect foreign capital inflows, we analyse direct penetration of foreign firms in the presence of oligopolistic interdependence between domestic and foreign firms. The existence of excess profits for domestic and foreign firms plays an important role to get the welfare effect of restrictions on foreign penetration.

In the analysis below we first show in section 3.2 that as long as the oligopolistic actions are strategic substitutes, there is a critical foreign

---

[2] See Hymer (1972).
[3] From chapter 6 onward we shall introduce the employment-generating effect of foreign direct investment. We shall also introduce a new approach to modelling foreign direct investment in chapter 7. A fuller discussion on the literature on foreign direct investment is postponed until then.
[4] See Bergsten, Horst and Moran (1978), Hood and Young (1979) and Hymer (1976, ch. 4).

share below which more restrictions on foreign direct penetration necessarily increase domestic total surplus. If the critical foreign share is rather small, this property may not be especially important to actual policy making. However, using a linear example, in section 3.3, we find that the critical foreign share can be surprisingly high.

Furthermore, in section 3.4, we show that restricting foreign direct penetration can increase domestic surplus even after compensating the foreign firm for the loss caused by the restriction especially when the foreign firm is not efficient enough. We also obtain some numerical values of the critical share for the foreign subsidiary firm below which more restrictions increase world surplus. In the analysis below, we mostly treat the case of foreign penetration through direct investment. However, section 3.5 notes that we can apply all our results to the case of quotas on foreign penetration through trade if the markets in the two countries are segmented. Finally, section 3.6 summarizes the results of the chapter and discusses some reservations of the analysis.

3.2   Foreign direct penetration and national welfare

Suppose that a foreign firm (or foreign firms) establishes a foreign subsidiary (or subsidiaries) and that direct investment cannot be replaced by trade. However, section 3.5 demonstrates that all results derived in sections 3.2–3.4 are still valid even in the case of foreign penetration through both trade and direct investment.

The domestic government is assumed to restrict the capacity of supply by the foreign subsidiary firm in order to protect domestic firms from the foreign penetration. Under perfect competition in the domestic market, such a quantitative restriction decreases domestic total surplus. The loss in domestic surplus is simply considered to be the costs for protecting domestic firms. However, in this chapter we find that the restriction against foreign penetration may increase domestic total surplus if the domestic market is oligopolistic.

Suppose that there are n domestic firms. The inverse demand function is given by

$$p = f(D), \text{ satisfying } f'(D) > 0, \tag{3.1}$$

where p and D denote price and demand, respectively. Profits π_i for a domestic firm i $(i = 1, \ldots, n)$ is represented by

$$\pi_i = f(D)x_i - c_i(x_i), \tag{3.2}$$

where x_i and $c_i(\cdot)$ represent the output and the total cost for firm i, respectively. Total demand D satisfies

$$D = \sum_{i=1}^{n} x_i + Q, \tag{3.3}$$

where Q represents the amount which the government permits the foreign (subsidiary) firm to supply.

In order to maximize π_i firm i determines x_i that satisfies

$$\frac{\partial \pi_i}{\partial x_i} = f(D) + f'(D)x_i(1 + \delta_i) - c_i'(x_i) = 0, \tag{3.4}$$

where δ_i, which represents firm i's conjectural variation of the rival firms' total output, is constant. If $\delta_i < -1$, each firm believes that it faces a positively sloped individual demand curve under which it can increase its profits as much as it wants simply by raising its price. If $\delta_i = -1$, perfect competition prevails. Therefore, in the following analysis we only deal with the case where

$$\delta_i > -1 \quad \text{for} \quad i = 1, \dots, n. \tag{3.5}$$

Needless to say, in the case of a Cournot oligopoly $\delta_i = 0$ for all i.

From (3.3) and (3.4), we find

$$\frac{dx_i}{dQ} = -\frac{f' + f''(D)x_i(1 + \delta_i)}{\{(1 + \delta_i)f' - c_i''\}\left[1 + \sum_j \frac{f' + f''(D)x_j(1+\delta_j)}{(1+\delta_j)f' - c_j''}\right]}$$

$$\frac{dp}{dQ} = \frac{f'}{1 + \sum_j \frac{f' + f''(D)x_j(1+\delta_j)}{(1+\delta_j)f' - c_j''}}.$$

Therefore,

$$\frac{dx_i}{dQ} < 0, \quad \frac{dp}{dQ} < 0, \tag{3.6}$$

if the demand function $f(\cdot)$ and the total cost function $c_i(\cdot)$ satisfy the following:

Assumption 3.1

$$f' + f''(D)x_i(1 + \delta_i) < 0, \quad (1 + \delta_i)f' - c_i'' < 0, \quad \text{for all } i.$$

The first property is a generalized version of assumption 2.1 in chapter 2. As stated just below assumption 2.1, this case corresponds to the 'normal' case in Seade (1980, pp. 483–4),[5] and to strategic substitutes in Bulow, Geanakoplos and Klemperer (1985).

[5] This first property is the same as Ruffin's assumption (1977), and the second is (5) in Seade (1980, p. 483). As Seade (1980, p. 484) states, the 'normal' property is satisfied unless the demand function is 'very' convex.

Since domestic producers' surplus W_p (the sum of the profits for all the domestic firms) is given by

$$W_p = \sum_i \{px_i - c_i(x_i)\}, \tag{3.7}$$

a change in W_p is derived as

$$dW_p = \sum_i \{p - c_i'(x_i)\}dx_i + \sum_i x_i dp. \tag{3.8}$$

On the other hand, as stated before, a change in consumers' surplus W_c is given by

$$dW_c = -Ddp. \tag{3.9}$$

Therefore, from (3.3), (3.4), (3.8) and (3.9), a change in domestic total surplus $W(= W_c + W_p)$ is calculated as

$$dW = \sum_i \{p - c_i'(x_i)\}dx_i - \left(D - \sum_i x_i\right)dp$$
$$= -\sum_i f'(D)(1 + \delta_i)x_i dx_i - Qdp. \tag{3.10}$$

In the case of perfect competition, p equals c_i'. Moreover, an increase in Q necessarily increases the total supply, and lowers p, see (3.6). Therefore, from (3.10) we obtain a well-known property for a competitive economy:

$$\frac{dW}{dQ} = -Q \cdot \frac{dp}{dQ} > 0 \quad \text{if and only if} \quad Q > 0.$$

It simply implies that the larger the foreign supply is, the greater surplus the host country obtains if the domestic market is competitive. However, if the domestic market is oligopolistic, the above property is not necessarily true. In fact, we prove the following proposition.

Proposition 3.1 *Suppose that the domestic government restricts a foreign (subsidiary) firm's output so as to protect domestic firms. Under the 'normal' conditions, given by assumption 3.1, there is a restriction level below which more restrictions on the foreign firm's supply always increase the total surplus of the host country.*

Proof. From (3.10) we get

$$\frac{dW}{dQ} = -\sum_i f'(D)(1 + \delta_i)x_i \frac{dx_i}{dQ} \quad \text{if} \quad Q = 0. \tag{3.11}$$

From (3.5), (3.6) and assumption 3.1, the right-hand side of (3.11) is negative. It implies that an increase in Q reduces domestic welfare W if Q is sufficiently small. Thus, there is some level of Q below which decreasing Q increases domestic total surplus W.   □

Let us intuitively explain the mechanism of this result. If the foreign firm's output is sufficiently small, the harmful effect of the price rise on the total surplus, $-Qdp$ in (3.10), caused by the restriction, is negligible. On the other hand, the beneficial effect of an increase in domestic firms' output is significant since there is a large discrepancy between the price and their marginal costs in the oligopolistic market.[6] Thus, if the government permits the foreign firm to supply only a small amount so as to protect domestic firms, more restrictions necessarily realize greater domestic surplus.

3.3   A linear demand case

Proposition 3.1 shows that, under a fairly general setup, more restrictions on foreign direct penetration increase domestic surplus when initially the government restricts the foreign share to a sufficiently low level. In this section we examine how small is the critical foreign share below which more restrictions on the foreign share increase domestic welfare. Obviously, the critical share depends on the shape of the demand function and that of each firm's cost function. In order to get some numerical values for the critical share, we assume a linear demand curve and constant marginal costs which may differ among firms. As we shall find out in the following analysis, the critical share is surprisingly high.

Let us assume that the domestic demand is given by

$$p = \alpha - \beta D, \tag{3.12}$$

and that the total cost for firm i is given by

$$c_i = \gamma_i x_i. \tag{3.13}$$

Substituting (3.12) and (3.13) into (3.4), and rearranging the terms, we get

$$x_i = \frac{\alpha - \gamma_i - \beta D}{\beta(1 + \delta_i)}. \tag{3.14}$$

---

[6] It is well known that promoting output by a monopoly firm by using subsidies increases total surplus. This is due to the existence of this discrepancy.

From (3.3) and (3.14), the equilibrium value of demand D is obtained as a function of Q:

$$D = F(Q) = \frac{\beta Q + \sum_i \frac{\alpha - \gamma_i}{1+\delta_i}}{\beta\{1 + \sum_i \frac{1}{1+\delta_i}\}}. \tag{3.15}$$

From (3.12), (3.13) and (3.14), total domestic surplus W in this case is

$$W = \int_0^{F(Q)} \beta\{F(Q) - D\} dD + \sum_i \{\alpha - \gamma_i - \beta F(Q)\} \cdot x_i$$

$$= \frac{\beta\{F(Q)\}^2}{2} + \sum_i \frac{\{\alpha - \gamma_i - \beta F(Q)\}^2}{\beta(1+\delta_i)}. \tag{3.16}$$

Using (3.15) and (3.16), we obtain

$$\frac{dW}{dQ} = \frac{2\beta F(Q)\left(\frac{Q}{F(Q)} - \frac{1}{2}\right)}{1 + \sum_i \frac{1}{1+\delta_i}}, \tag{3.17}$$

and it can be easily shown that

$$\frac{d^2 W}{dQ^2} = \frac{\beta\{1 + 2\sum_i \frac{1}{1+\delta_i}\}}{\{1 + \sum_i \frac{1}{1+\delta_i}\}^2} > 0. \tag{3.18}$$

From (3.17) and (3.18), it follows that domestic surplus W is a U-shaped function of the foreign firm's supply Q. It also follows from (3.17) that the domestic surplus is lowest when the foreign share, $Q/F(Q)$, is 50%,[7] though the market looks most competitive at that share. If the foreign share is lower than 50%, decreasing the foreign share necessarily increases the domestic surplus.[8]

Since W is a U-shaped function of Q, if the present foreign share is smaller than a certain critical level, the total prohibition against foreign production realizes the highest surplus for the host country. Let us next examine how high this critical foreign share ($\hat{\sigma}$) is. For that purpose, we

---

[7] Analysing the effect of changes in the number of foreign firms under symmetric Cournot oligopoly through trade, Dixit (1984) found that a decrease in the number of foreign firms increases domestic welfare if the foreign share is less than 50% under the linearity assumption. The present result generalizes his result to the case where marginal costs and conjectural variations are different among firms.

[8] If $\delta_j = -1$ (namely, under perfect competition), the price is equal to the lowest of the marginal costs among domestic firms, and since we here treat the case where the marginal cost is constant, the price is also constant. Obviously, Q does not affect the domestic surplus in this case.

calculate total demand $\hat{D}$ that satisfies

$$
\begin{aligned}
W &= \frac{\beta \hat{D}^2}{2} + \sum_i \frac{(\alpha - \gamma_i - \beta \hat{D})^2}{\beta(1 + \delta_i)} \\
&= \frac{\beta \{F(0)\}^2}{2} + \sum_i \frac{\{\alpha - \gamma_i - \beta F(0)\}^2}{\beta(1 + \delta_i)},
\end{aligned}
\tag{3.19}
$$

where $F(0)$ represents the total demand (= output) under the total prohibition against the foreign penetration, as is seen from (3.15). It is to be noted that in (3.19) $\hat{D}$ stands for the total demand (= output) when the foreign share has critical level $\hat{\sigma}$. From (3.15) and (3.19), we get

$$
\hat{D} = \frac{\sum_i \frac{\alpha - \gamma_i}{\beta(1 + \delta_i)} \cdot \{3 + 2 \sum_i \frac{1}{1 + \delta_i}\}}{\{1 + \sum_i \frac{1}{1 + \delta_i}\}\{1 + 2 \sum_i \frac{1}{1 + \delta_i}\}}.
\tag{3.20}
$$

From (3.15) we obtain the foreign supply $\hat{Q}$ at which the total demand becomes $\hat{D}$, i.e., $\hat{D} = F(\hat{Q})$. Therefore, using (3.15) and (3.20) we find critical foreign share $\hat{\sigma}$:

$$
\begin{aligned}
\hat{\sigma} &= \frac{\hat{Q}}{\hat{D}} = \left\{ 1 + \sum_i \frac{1}{1 + \delta_i} \right\} - \frac{\sum_i \frac{\alpha - \gamma_i}{\beta(1 + \delta_i)}}{\hat{D}} \\
&= \frac{2 \left\{ 1 + \sum_i \frac{1}{1 + \delta_i} \right\}}{3 + 2 \sum_i \frac{1}{1 + \delta_i}}.
\end{aligned}
\tag{3.21}
$$

Since (3.5) implies $\sum (1/(1 + \delta_i)) > 0$, from (3.21) $\hat{\sigma}$ is found to satisfy

$$
\hat{\sigma} > \frac{2}{3}.
$$

Note that $\hat{\sigma}$ does not depend on the distribution of marginal costs among oligopolists; it only depends on the values of conjectural variations δ_i's.[9]

We summarize the above results in the following proposition.

Proposition 3.2 *Under a linear demand curve and constant marginal costs for domestic firms, we get the following properties for any value of conjectural variations (as long as $\delta_j > -1$) and for any distribution of marginal costs among domestic firms:*
(1) Domestic total surplus is lowest when the foreign share is restricted to 50%.
(2) If the host country only permits the foreign (subsidiary) firm to have a share smaller than 2/3 (= 67%), a total prohibition against the foreign penetration realizes the highest domestic surplus.

[9] It can be verified in the same way as above that if the marginal cost is linearly decreasing, the critical foreign share is higher than the case where the marginal costs are constant.

Table 3.1 *Critical shares
for welfare-improving
elimination of foreign
penetration*

n	$\hat{\sigma}$ (in %)
1	80
2	86
3	89
4	91
5	92

In the special case of Cournot oligopoly, it follows from (3.21) that

$$\hat{\sigma} = \frac{2(n + 1)}{2n + 3}. \tag{3.22}$$

The critical share only depends on the number of domestic firms (n) although the domestic firms have different market shares because of the difference in marginal costs among them. Some examples of the combination of the number of domestic firms and the critical foreign share are given in table 3.1. Figure 3.1 gives the relationship between the market share of foreign firms and domestic welfare. As can be seen from figure 3.1, domestic welfare is minimized when foreign share is 50%, and the critical foreign share $\hat{\sigma}$ is greater than 67%.

It is reasonable to assume that some domestic firms may not survive when the foreign share is very high such as 89% in the case of domestic triopoly (see table 3.1). As long as the domestic government disapproves such a high foreign share so as to protect domestic firms, a total prohibition against foreign direct penetration benefits the country most.

3.4   Effect on world welfare

The previous section has shown that a further restriction on foreign direct penetration is advantageous to the host country if the government controls the initial amount of foreign supply to a sufficiently low level so as to protect domestic firms. Since the foreign firm loses profit opportunities under the restriction, it is a beggar-thy-neighbour policy. However, if the restriction increases world surplus, including foreign profits, the domestic country can be better off even after a full compensation for the loss by foreign firms. In fact, we can find the condition under which a restriction on foreign supply increases world surplus.

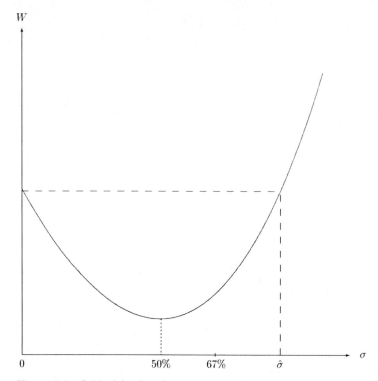

Figure 3.1 Critical foreign shares

Producers' surplus (= profits) for the foreign subsidiary firm is

$$W_f = pQ - c_f(Q),$$ (3.23)

where $c_f(\cdot)$ represents the cost function for the foreign firm. From (3.3), (3.10) and (3.23), the effect of changes in Q on world surplus $W^*(= W + W_f)$ is

$$\frac{dW^*}{dQ} = \sum_i (p - c_i'(x_i))\frac{dx_i}{dQ} + p - c_f'(Q).$$ (3.24)

Using (3.6) and (3.24), we find that

$$\frac{dW^*}{dQ} < 0 \quad \text{if} \quad p - c_f'(Q) \approx 0.$$ (3.25)

This implies that restricting output of the foreign subsidiary firm increases the world surplus if the difference between the price and marginal costs for the foreign firm is sufficiently small.[10] We summarize the above results as follows.

Proposition 3.3 *If the difference between the price and marginal costs for a foreign (subsidiary) firm is sufficiently small, restricting its output benefits the host country even after compensating the foreign firm for losses caused by the restriction.*

Let us next investigate the critical foreign share at which the restriction increases the world total surplus. If the critical share is very small, the policy implications of this proposition is of little interest. Generally, the critical share depends on the shape of the cost and demand functions, the number of domestic firms, and conjectural variations. In order to get an intuitive figure for the critical share, we assume a Cournot oligopoly ($\delta_j = 0$) and use the linear example presented in the previous section.

We get three kinds of critical foreign shares, σ_1, σ_2 and σ_3, explained below. In the analysis here we assume that there is no initial restriction on the level of foreign supply, i.e., Q is endogenously determined in the market. Foreign share σ_1 is defined as the foreign share below which a marginal reduction in Q increases world surplus as well as domestic surplus. If the foreign share is less than σ_2, a total prohibition gives greater world surplus than that under the free-market equilibrium. Finally, if the foreign share is less than σ_3, a total prohibition against foreign penetration maximizes world surplus.

Analogous to (3.14), in the absence of any restriction of foreign supply, the optimal supply $\bar{Q}$ for the foreign subsidiary firm satisfies

$$\bar{Q} = \frac{\alpha - \gamma_f - \beta D}{\beta}, \tag{3.26}$$

where γ_f is the constant marginal cost for the firm. From (3.15) and (3.26), $\bar{Q}$ is solved as

$$\bar{Q} = \frac{(\alpha - \gamma_f)(n + 1) - \sum_i(\alpha - \gamma_i)}{\beta(n + 2)}. \tag{3.27}$$

If the foreign supply is restricted to a level lower than this, the restriction is clearly effective.

By applying function $F(Q)$ defined in (3.15) to the sum of (3.16) and (3.23) in which $c_f = \gamma_f Q$ we obtain world surplus W^* as a function

---

[10] The analysis in chapter 1 can be interpreted as being that of world welfare in the presence of foreign ownership of some of the firms there. Since this model here assumes general conjectural variations, it is an extension of the analysis of chapter 1.

of Q:

$$W^*(Q) = A - \frac{\beta Q^2}{2(n+1)^2} \tag{3.28}$$
$$+ \left[\alpha - \gamma_f - \frac{(n+2)\sum_i(\alpha - \gamma_i)}{(n+1)^2} \right] Q,$$

where A represents the following constant value:

$$A = (1+\beta)\left[\sum_i(\alpha - \gamma_i)^2 - \left\{ \frac{n + \frac{3}{2}}{(n+1)^2} \right\} \left\{ \sum_i(\alpha - \gamma_i) \right\}^2 \right].$$

From (3.28), we get

$$W^{*\prime}(Q) = \alpha - \gamma_f - \frac{\beta Q + (n+2)\sum_i(\alpha - \gamma_i)}{(n+1)^2}, \tag{3.29}$$
$$W^{*\prime\prime}(Q) < 0.$$

From (3.15), foreign share σ can be obtained as a function of Q. In particular,

$$\sigma(Q) = \frac{Q}{F(Q)} = \frac{n+1}{1 + \sum_i \frac{\alpha - \gamma_i}{\beta Q}}. \tag{3.30}$$

If $W^{*\prime}(\bar{Q}) < 0$, a marginal restriction on foreign supply increases the world surplus. From (3.27) and (3.29), the condition for $W^{*\prime}(\bar{Q}) < 0$ is

$$(n+1)(\alpha - \gamma_f) < \frac{n^2 + 4n + 3}{n^2 + 3n + 1} \cdot \sum_i(\alpha - \gamma_i).$$

Then, from (3.27) we get

$$\frac{\sum_i(\alpha - \gamma_i)}{\beta \bar{Q}} > n^2 + 3n + 1. \tag{3.31}$$

Therefore, from (3.30) and (3.31), it follows that

$$\sigma(\bar{Q}) < \frac{1}{n+2} \equiv \sigma_1. \tag{3.32}$$

It implies that if the foreign share at the equilibrium is lower than the right-hand side of (3.32), a marginal reduction in the foreign supply increases the world surplus since $W^{*\prime}(\bar{Q}) < 0$. The right-hand side of (3.32) is defined to be σ_1.

Turning to the definition of σ_2, if the world surplus is lower in the no-restriction equilibrium than under a total prohibition on foreign supply, we must have

$$W^*(0) > W^*(\bar{Q}),$$

which, because of (3.27) and (3.28), is equivalent to the condition

$$(n+1)(\alpha - \gamma_f) < \frac{2n^2 + 8n + 7}{2n^2 + 6n + 3} \cdot \sum_i (\alpha - \gamma_i).$$

Using this inequality and (3.27), we obtain

$$\sum_i \frac{\alpha - \gamma_i}{\beta \bar{Q}} > \frac{2n^2 + 6n + 3}{2}. \tag{3.33}$$

From (3.30) and (3.33), we find that if σ satisfies

$$\sigma < \frac{n+1}{n^2 + 3n + \frac{5}{2}} \equiv \sigma_2, \tag{3.34}$$

a total prohibition on foreign supply yields higher world surplus than under the no-restriction equilibrium.

Finally, we derive σ_3. From (3.29), we know that $W^{*\prime\prime}(Q) < 0$. Therefore if $W^{*\prime}(0) < 0$, then $W^{*\prime}(Q) < 0$ for all $Q (\geqslant 0)$. From this property, we conclude that a total prohibition against foreign penetration always attains the highest world surplus if $W^{*\prime}(0) < 0$. From (3.29), the condition that $W^{*\prime}(0) < 0$ is represented as

$$(n+1)(\alpha - \gamma_f) < \frac{n+2}{n+1} \cdot \sum_i (\alpha - \gamma_i).$$

Therefore, from (3.27), we get

$$\sum_i \frac{\alpha - \gamma_i}{\beta \bar{Q}} > (n+1)(n+2). \tag{3.35}$$

Finally, from (3.30) and (3.35), we obtain

$$\sigma < \frac{n+1}{n^2 + 3n + 3} \equiv \sigma_3. \tag{3.36}$$

Note that all three critical shares σ_i ($i = 1, 2$ and 3) are smaller than $\hat{\sigma}$ given by (3.22). Therefore, restricting the foreign supply necessarily increases domestic surplus W if the foreign share under the no-restriction equilibrium is smaller than σ_i's ($i = 1, 2$ and 3).

Table 3.2 presents σ_1, σ_2 and σ_3 for various levels of n. In the case where there are two domestic firms, for example, if the foreign share without restrictions is smaller than 25%, a marginal restriction on the foreign supply increases not only domestic surplus W but also world surplus W^*. If the share is smaller than 24%, the total prohibition yields

Table 3.2 *Various critical shares with foreign penetration*

n	σ_1 (in %)	σ_2 (in %)	σ_3 (in %)
1	33.3	30.8	28.6
2	25.0	24.0	23.1
3	20.0	19.5	19.0
4	16.7	16.4	16.1
5	14.3	14.1	14.0
6	12.5	12.4	12.3
7	11.1	11.0	11.0

higher world surplus than that which is obtained in the no-restriction equilibrium. Furthermore, if the foreign share is smaller than 23.1%, not only domestic surplus but also world surplus becomes highest under the total prohibition.

Note that σ_1 equals $\tilde{\sigma}$ presented in table 1.3 and that σ_2 equals $\bar{\sigma}$ in table 1.2. In the closed-economy setting of chapter 1 if a firm's share is lower than $\tilde{\sigma}$, a marginal production tax on it raises national welfare. Since the same property holds for the effect of an exogenous decrease in the firm's supply on world welfare in the present setting, σ_1 is the same as $\tilde{\sigma}$. Since removing a firm whose share is less than σ_2 benefits the country in a closed-economy setting, it is the same as σ_2 in a world-economy setting.

3.5   Penetration through trade

Since we have so far treated the case of non-tradeable goods, we have not considered the possibility of trade. However, our results are also valid in the case of foreign penetration through trade and/or direct foreign investment under some conditions.[11] First, as long as the markets in the two countries are segmented, we can obtain the same equations as (3.3)–(3.11) by replacing the foreign subsidiary production Q by the sum of foreign subsidiary production and imports. Therefore, proposition 3.1 can be directly applied to the case of foreign penetration through trade and direct investment. For example, by restricting the total foreign supply the domestic country can increase total domestic surplus if the foreign share is small enough.

Besides the segmentation of the market, we also need the assumption that the foreign firm's marginal costs of supply to its own country are

[11] It will be shown in chapter 6 that in the presence of unemployment the results can be very different between penetration by foreign direct investment and by exports.

not affected by changes in exports. This may be the case for an industry where various specifications differ internationally and thus firms have to establish independent production facilities for domestic and foreign use. In this case total domestic surplus is not affected by changes in total supply (viz., exports plus subsidiary production) to foreign countries. We obtain the same equations as (3.23)–(3.25) by considering Q as the sum of imports and foreign subsidiary production and that $c_f(Q)$ is the total cost under the optimal allocation of production Q between the two countries. Therefore, proposition 3.3 is extended to the case of foreign penetration through trade and/or direct investment. If the foreign firm is not efficient enough, restricting foreign penetration through trade and/or direct investment can increase even the world total surplus.[12]

In contrast, if the foreign firm uses the same facilities for domestic and foreign supply, the total surplus in the foreign market is affected by an import quota imposed by the domestic country since changes in exports under the quota vary the foreign firm's marginal cost of supply to its own country. However, this effect makes the result stated in proposition 3.3 even stronger if the marginal cost is increasing in output. Reductions in exports lower the marginal cost since the total supply decreases. Therefore, an import quota increases not only domestic total surplus plus foreign profits in the domestic country but also total surplus in the foreign country if the foreign share in the domestic country is small enough.

3.6   Conclusion

Restricting output by a foreign subsidiary firm in an oligopolistic market raises the domestic price and increases domestic firms' output. Consequently, consumers' surplus declines and the domestic producers' surplus rises. If the output of the domestic firms were invariant, the beneficial effect of the (marginal) price rise on the domestic firms' profits would be smaller than the harmful effect on consumers' surplus by the amount of foreign supply at the price. Therefore, the lower the output the foreign firm produces, the smaller becomes the harmful effect of the price rise.

Besides the price effect, the restriction increases outputs of the domestic firms, and hence increases domestic producers' surplus. If the market is competitive, this effect is negligible since the price then equals the marginal cost. Under oligopoly, in contrast, the increase in producers' surplus is significant since the price is higher than the marginal cost.

---

[12] Obviously, under the Heckscher-Ohlin framework less efficient foreign firms cannot survive. However, in the case of oligopoly in the segmented market with a fixed number of firms, foreign firms can export to the domestic market even if they are less efficient.

Therefore, under oligopoly if the foreign share is smaller than a certain critical level, the harmful effect of the price rise caused by the restriction is dominated by the beneficial effect of the increase in the domestic firms' profits. In other words, restricting small-scale foreign penetration necessarily increases domestic surplus. The critical share is found to be surprisingly high. Furthermore, the restriction may even increase world total surplus. The host country may be able to benefit even after compensating the foreign firm for the loss caused by the restriction. It occurs especially when the foreign subsidiary is much less efficient than domestic firms. This is because under such circumstances the restriction reallocates production from the less efficient firm (the foreign subsidiary) to the more efficient ones (domestic firms). This property is a direct application of the result of chapter 1 to an international context.

It is also to be noted that most of the results can be applied to the case of foreign penetration through trade and direct investment, especially when the market is segmented between the two countries.

We conclude this chapter by noting some reservations about the present analysis. In this chapter we assume that each firm does not change conjectural variations under a restriction on foreign penetration. In the case of Cournot oligopoly a restriction on foreign penetration does not affect conjectural variations with respect to foreign supply since reactions by rival firms are taken to be invariant even without quantitative restrictions. Even under general conjectural variations, given that the domestic government imposes a restriction on the foreign supply, domestic firms do not change conjectural variations since the foreign supply is fixed. Therefore, we can apply the present results to the analysis of the effect of changes in the restriction level.

However, in the case of general conjectural variations, imposing quantitative restrictions on the foreign supply itself may affect conjectural variations and vary the equilibrium. This effect should be taken into account when we compare surplus under a total prohibition with that under totally free foreign penetration.

Also, the present results are obtained on the assumption that the number of domestic firms is fixed. In the case of free entry and exit by domestic firms, the profits of domestic firms are zero and the price does not change. Therefore, changes in the restriction level affect neither consumers' surplus nor producers' surplus in the host country. However, owing to the uneven distribution of technology among firms, the existence of various entry barriers, etc., it is not realistic to assume that the profits of domestic firms are zero. If domestic firms earn some profits, the present mechanism works and then there is a possibility that restricting foreign penetration increases national welfare.

4　Trade and industrial policy under asymmetric oligopoly: a synthesis

4.1　Introduction

Chapters 1 and 3 investigated the welfare effect of various policies that restrict a firm's production, such as a production tax-cum-subsidy and removal of a firm in a closed- and an open-economy context. In both chapters the existence of cost asymmetry played an important role. This chapter provides a general model that synthesizes those two models. It also synthesizes various models in the literature on trade and industrial policies in oligopolistic markets.

The literature on international trade with international oligopolistic interdependence in production is voluminous and various issues have been discussed.[1] The question of appropriate and strategic trade and industrial policies becomes an obvious target for analysis in models with oligopolistic industries. Optimal R&D policies – see, for example, Lahiri and Ono (1999b), Spence (1984) and Spencer and Brander (1983) – entry–exit policies – see, for example, Dixit (1984), Lahiri and Ono (1988), Okuno-Fujiwara and Suzumura (1993), Ono (1990) and Suzumura and Kiyono (1987) – and the optimal trade policy in an oligopolistic market with and without free entry – see, for example, Brander and Spencer (1985), Eaton and Grossman (1992), Hortsmann and Markusen (1986), Markusen and Venables (1988) and Venables (1985) – have all received quite a lot of attention in the literature.

Previous analyses on tax policies have considered across-the-board taxes or subsidies under either the assumption that the number of firms is fixed or that there is completely free entry and exit.[2] Similar comments also apply to the literature on other forms of industrial policies. There is another important factor that divides the literature into two groups:

---

[1] See Brander (1995) for a survey of the literature.
[2] Lahiri and Ono (1995b) extend the standard 2x2 Heckscher-Ohlin model into a model in which one of the two sectors is characterized by a Cournot oligopoly and show that many of the well-known results in trade models with no-entry oligopoly do not go through under free entry.

whereas Lahiri and Ono (1988 and 1997) and Ono (1990) treat the case of cost asymmetry among oligopolists within a country, the others assume all domestic oligopolists to be identical.

This chapter presents a general model that nests all the papers cited above. In this way we are able to generalize many of the results on the welfare effects of entry–exit policies. We focus directly on the number of firms and on the issue of elimination of a marginal firm. In this sense this chapter slots in between the no-entry oligopoly model and the free-entry ones.

After the general model is presented in section 4.2, section 4.3 obtains a number of general results on the welfare effect of removing a firm. Section 4.4 assumes the demand function to be linear and derives more specific results than the ones obtained in the preceding sections. For example, we obtain specific values for the critical share of a firm below which the firm should be removed. The possibility of foreign ownership of firms and how it affects the results are discussed in section 4.5. Welfare effects of discriminatory production subsidies are analysed in section 4.6. Finally, section 4.7 summarizes the main contributions of this chapter.

4.2   The framework of analysis

We consider a partial equilibrium model with a homogeneous commodity. There are m countries and n^j firms in country j ($j = 1, \ldots, m$).[3] The international market for this commodity is assumed to be integrated. All the firms are Cournot oligopolists and have constant (though different) marginal costs. The marginal cost of the ith firm in the jth country is denoted by c_i^j ($i = 1, \ldots, n^j$ and $j = 1, \ldots, m$). World demand and demand originating from country j are respectively D and D^j. The inverse demand function is given by

$$p = f(D), \tag{4.1}$$

where p is the price of the commodity.

Profits for the ith firm in the jth country, π_i^j, are

$$\pi_i^j = \left(f(D) - c_i^j + s_i^j\right)x_i^j, \tag{4.2}$$

where x_i^j and s_i^j are respectively the output of, and the specific subsidy to, the firm. For the clearance of the international commodity market we

---

[3] We shall extend the analysis to the case where some firms in a country may be owned by some other country (or countries).

must have

$$D = \sum_{j=1}^{m} \sum_{i=1}^{n^j} x_i^j. \tag{4.3}$$

Each firm maximizes its profits, taking the output of all other firms as given. Using (4.2) and (4.3) we obtain the first-order profit maximization condition:

$$f(D) + f'(D)x_i^j = c_i^j - s_i^j. \tag{4.4}$$

We impose the standard assumption with respect to demand, which is the same as (1.3) in chapter 1.

Assumption 4.1

$$f'(D) < 0 \text{ and } f'(D) + x_i^j f''(D) < 0 \text{ for all } D \geq x_i^j \geq 0.$$

Each country's welfare is assumed to be the sum of producers' and consumers' surplus minus subsidy payments in the country. That is, the welfare of country j, W^j, is

$$W^j = \sum_{i=1}^{n^j} \pi_i^j + CS^j - \sum_{i=1}^{n^j} s_i^j x_i^j, \tag{4.5}$$

where CS^j is the consumers' surplus in country j. It can be easily shown that

$$dCS^j = -D^j dp. \tag{4.6}$$

This completes the description of the formal framework of our analysis. We shall now conclude this section by noting that the models of chapters 1 and 3 and many existing models in the literature are special cases of the above framework. First of all, when the number of countries is unity, i.e., $m = 1$, the above model reduces to the one analysed in chapter 1 (see also Lahiri and Ono, 1988). This is the closed-economy case. Furthermore, Suzumura and Kiyono (1987) consider the case of symmetric oligopoly in a closed economy, i.e., $m = 1$ and $c_i^1 = c_k^1$ for all i and k. A two-country model with symmetric oligopolists – $m = 2$, and for each j, $c_i^j = c_k^j$ for all i and k – is analysed by Dixit (1984). The model of direct foreign investment discussed in chapter 3 (see also Ono, 1990) is a special case with $m = 2$ and $D^2 = 0$. That is, in the model of chapter 3 the entire demand comes only from the home country. Brander and Spencer (1985) analyse an international duopoly model in which there are three countries two of which produce only for consumption in the third country, i.e., $m = 3$, $n^1 = n^2 = 1$, $n^3 = 0$, and $D^1 = D^2 = 0$. Finally, Lahiri and

Ono (1995a) extend the Brander and Spencer (1985) framework to allow for multiple asymmetric oligopolists in one of the countries, i.e., $m = 3$, $n^1 = 2$, $n^2 = 1$, $n^3 = 0$, and $D^1 = D^2 = 0$.

4.3   Entry–exit policy and welfare

In this section we shall analyse the effect of an exogenous rise in the marginal cost of one of the firms in a country on the welfare levels of the domestic and foreign countries. As shown in chapters 1 and 3, an exogenous rise in the marginal cost may well benefit the domestic country. This section also shows that there is a case where it makes the foreign countries better off. Some particular conditions with respect to the trade pattern are needed for these properties to be valid in the present general framework. Moreover, these results are applied to the analysis of the welfare effect of an elimination policy.

We first of all establish the relationship between the marginal cost of one firm and the welfare level of each country. Without any loss of generality, we analyse the welfare effects of changes in the marginal cost of firm 1 in country 1, dW^j/dc_1^1 $(j = 1, \ldots, m)$, under the assumption that there are no production taxes or subsidies, i.e., $s_i^j = 0$ for all i and j. The welfare effect of a production tax will be analysed in section 4.6.

By totally differentiating (4.2) and (4.5) and using (4.4) and (4.6), we obtain a very general expression for a change in each country's welfare, as stated below.

Theorem 1

$$dW^j = (-f') \left(\sum_{i=1}^{n^j} x_i^j dx_i^j - e^j dD \right) \quad (for\ j = 2, \ldots, m)$$

(4.7)

and $\quad dW^1 = (-f') \left(\sum_{i=1}^{n^1} x_i^1 dx_i^1 - e^1 dD \right) - x_1^1 dc_1^1,$ (4.8)

where e^j is the level of exports by country j, i.e.,

$$e^j = \sum_{i=1}^{n^j} x_i^j - D^j.$$

(4.9)

The cross welfare effect in (4.7) is decomposed into two terms: the oligopoly effect and the terms of trade effect. The terms of trade effect is represented by $f'e^j dD$ and the rest stands for the oligopoly effect.

The own welfare effect, given in (4.8), has an additional effect: the direct cost-reducing effect $(-x_1^1 dc_1^1)$.

In appendix A we have proved that under assumption 4.1

$$\frac{dx_i^j}{dc_1^1} \begin{cases} < 0 & \text{if } i = j = 1 \\ > 0 & \text{otherwise} \end{cases}$$

and $\quad \dfrac{dD}{dc_1^1} < 0.$ \hfill (4.10)

Since from (4.10) a rise in the marginal cost of a firm decreases its own, and increases all the other firms', production, the market share of the firm monotonically declines as its marginal cost rises. Thus, in our framework, a firm with a sufficiently high (low) marginal cost is a minor (major) firm. Using equation (4.10), a number of implications of the above theorem are derived in the following propositions the proofs of which are given in appendix B.

Proposition 4.1 *An increase in the marginal costs of, or elimination of, a minor firm in a country unambiguously benefits the country if it is an exporter (or even a minor importer) of the commodity, and harms the country if its total domestic production is much smaller than its demand. If there is only one significant producer in a country and its marginal cost increases, the country is unambiguously worse off.*

Proposition 4.2 *If all firms in a country are identical, an increase in the marginal costs of one of the firms unambiguously harms the country.*

Proposition 4.3 *An increase in the marginal costs of a firm, or elimination of it, in a country benefits other countries if they are exporters (or even minor importers), and harms them if in those countries domestic production is much smaller than domestic demand. These properties hold irrespective of whether the firm is minor, major or identical to all the other firms in the country.*

Intuitively, an increase in the marginal costs of a firm in country 1 raises the price of the commodity. Therefore, all exporters benefit from the improved terms of trade and all importers lose from it. Moreover, an increase in the marginal costs of one firm raises the profits of the other firms. Since the profits of the firm whose marginal costs increase go down, total profits in country 1 will go up (down) if the firm is a minor (major) one. Total profits in the other countries go up. Thus, the exporting countries other than country 1 gain on all counts: an improvement in the terms of trade and an increase in profits. The importing countries, on the other hand, lose out from deteriorating terms of trade and this loss outweighs the increase in profits if they are not major producers. Country 1 is better off if it is an exporter and the firm whose marginal costs have increased is a minor firm. If, on the other hand, this firm is the only major firm in country 1, then this country is unambiguously worse off. This is because the loss of profits will either dominate the gain from improved terms of trade (if the country is an exporter) or reinforce the loss from deteriorating terms of trade (if the country is an importer).

We shall demonstrate how some of the existing results are special cases of the above three propositions. First of all, in chapter 1 (see also Lahiri and Ono, 1988) we consider the special case of a closed economy, i.e., $m = 1$, and show that eliminating a minor firm unambiguously benefits the country. Dixit (1984) assumes that $m = 2$, $D^2 = 0$ and $c_i^j = c_k^j$ for all i, k and j, and finds that decreasing the number of firms in country 2 may improve country 1's welfare. Chapter 3 of this book (see also Ono, 1990) considers the case where $m = 2$, $D^2 = 0$ and the firms in country 1 are not necessarily symmetric. It derives that eliminating a foreign firm may well raise the welfare of country 1. Finally, in Lahiri and Ono (1995a) $m = 3$, $n^1 = 2$, $n^2 = 1$, $n^3 = 0$, and $D^1 = D^2 = 0$. In this case, if the firm whose marginal costs decline is a minor firm in country 1, countries 1 and 2 are unambiguously worse off and country 3 is better off. If the firm is a major one, the country where that firm is located is better off and the other two countries are unambiguously worse off. These results are special cases of propositions 4.1 and 4.3.

We conclude this section by noting that eliminating a minor firm in any country will enhance the total surplus of the world.[4] This can easily be derived by summing over the welfare equations in (4.7) and (4.8).

4.4   Critical shares in the linear case

In proposition 4.1 we have shown that elimination of a 'minor' firm benefits the country if it is an exporter and harms it if its total domestic production is 'not very large'. However, we have not yet established exactly how minor the firm should be for the result to hold. Nor have we explained what we mean exactly by 'much smaller'. This section assumes linear demand, i.e., $f'' = 0$, and obtains the critical share of a firm in the country's total production below which the firm should be removed.

---

[4] This result is essentially the same as obtained in chapter 1 (see also Lahiri and Ono, 1988).

When $f'' = 0$, equations (A.4.2) and (A.4.3) in appendix A reduce to

$$\frac{dx_i^j}{dc_1^1} = \begin{cases} \frac{N}{(N+1)f'} & \text{if } i = j = 1 \\[2ex] -\frac{1}{(N+1)f'} & \text{otherwise} \end{cases}$$

and $$\frac{dD}{dc_1^1} = \frac{1}{(N+1)f'}. \tag{4.11}$$

Substituting the above expressions into (4.7) and (4.8) yields

$$(N+1)\frac{dW^j}{dc_1^1} = \begin{cases} X^1 + e^1 - 2(N+1)x_1^1 & \text{if } j = 1 \\[2ex] X^j + e^j & \text{otherwise} \end{cases}$$

where $$X^j = \sum_{i=1}^{n_j} x_i^j. \tag{4.12}$$

Since the domestic firms' share in country j's domestic market, $\sigma_d^j (= X^j/D^j)$, satisfies

$$X^j + e^j = D^j (2\sigma_d^j - 1), \tag{4.13}$$

from (4.12), we find

$$\frac{dW^1}{dc_1^1} \gtreqless 0 \quad \text{if} \quad \frac{x_1^1}{X^1} \lesseqgtr \frac{1 + \frac{e^1}{X^1}}{2(N+1)},$$

$$\frac{dW^j}{dc_1^1} \gtreqless 0 \quad \text{if} \quad \sigma_d^j (= X^j/D^j) \gtreqless \frac{1}{2} \quad \text{for} \quad j \neq 1. \tag{4.14}$$

This property shows the critical shares related to propositions 4.1 and 4.3; that is, (1) the share of a firm in a country below which an increase in the firm's marginal cost benefits that country, and (2) the share of domestic firms in the domestic market above which an increase in a foreign firm's marginal costs benefits the country.

Proposition 4.4 *When the demand function is linear, an increase in the marginal costs of a firm, say firm 1 in country 1, benefits its own country if and only if*

$$\frac{x_1^1}{X^1} < \frac{1 + \frac{e^1}{X^1}}{2(N+1)}.$$

It benefits other countries if their domestic firms' share in each domestic market is more than 50%, and harms them if the share is less than 50%. When the share is exactly 50%, the welfare level is lowest in those countries.[5]

---

[5] This result is essentially the same as the first property of proposition 3.2 in chapter 3.

This proposition implies that an increase in the marginal costs of a firm in a country (say, country 1) with no domestic demand ($e^1 = X^1$) benefits the country if and only if the share of that firm in the domestic production of the commodity (x_1^1 / X^1) is less than $1/(N+1)$. For example, if there are three firms in the world, a reduction in the marginal costs of a firm which produces less than a quarter of domestic production harms the country.

Having considered the welfare effects of small changes in the marginal costs of a firm, we now turn to the welfare effect of eliminating a firm. In particular, we shall find out the following critical share: if a firm's share is below the critical share then eliminating it makes the country better off.

As before suppose that firm 1 in country 1 is under consideration for elimination. Let $W^1(x_1^1)$ denote the welfare of country 1 where firm 1 produces x_1^1. When the world inverse demand function is of the form:

$$p = \alpha - \beta D, \tag{4.15}$$

and the share of country 1 in world demand is constant (denoted by γ^1),[6] $W^1(x_1^1)$ is represented by (details in appendix C)

$$W^1(x_1^1) = (x_1^1)^2 \beta \left(3 - \frac{2(n^1 - 1) + \gamma^1}{2N^2} \right) - \frac{x_1^1 \beta (e^1 + X^1)}{N} + \theta, \tag{4.16}$$

where θ is a term which depends only on the parameters of the model and not on any of the variables. Thus, $W^1(x_1^1)$ is a U-shaped function of x_1^1.[7] In order to obtain the critical share we find critical output x^* that satisfies

$$W^1(x^*) = W^1(0). \tag{4.17}$$

From (4.16) and (4.17), the critical value for x_1^1 is solved to be

$$x_1^{1*} = \frac{N(e^1 + X^1)}{(N+1)^2 - n^1 - \frac{\gamma^1}{2}}.$$

From the above result we obtain the critical share below which a firm should be eliminated (discussed in proposition 4.1).

---

[6] This assumption, which is valid when all consumers in the world are homogeneous, is made for computational simplicity. Its relaxation creates unrewarding complications.

[7] This is so since the coefficient of $(x_1^1)^2$ in the expression for $W^1(x_1^1)$ is positive and that for x_1^1 is negative (as long as $e^1 + X^1 > 0$). In other words, the slope of function $W^1(\cdot)$ is negative to start with and positive for large values for x_1^1.

Proposition 4.5 *In the case of linear demand eliminating a firm in a country – say firm 1 in country 1 – increases country 1's welfare if and only if*

$$\frac{x_1^1}{X^1} < \frac{N\left(1 + \frac{e^1}{X^1}\right)}{(N+1)^2 - n^1 - \frac{\gamma^1}{2}}.$$

Proposition 4.5 generalizes the results of chapter 1 (see also Lahiri and Ono, 1988) and Dixit (1984). The former obtained the critical shares for the linear case in a closed economy with asymmetric oligopoly and the latter for an open economy with symmetric oligopoly within each country.

A number of interesting special cases of the above result can now be derived. First of all, if σ_d^1 (the share of the domestic firms in the domestic market) is less than 50%, (i.e., $e^1 + X^1 < 0$ from (4.13), the inequality in proposition 4.5 never holds and, thus, eliminating a domestic firm will always harm the country.[8]

Second, when only two domestic and one foreign firms – $N = 3$ and $n^1 = 2$ – compete just for the domestic market (i.e., $\gamma^1 = 1$), a domestic firm should be eliminated if its market share is less than 0.44 $(0.5 - \sigma_f)$ where $\sigma_f = (D^1 - X^1)/D^1$ denotes the market share of the foreign firm. In particular, if the share of the foreign firm is 25%, the critical market share for the domestic firm to be eliminated is 11.11%.

Third, when $N = n^1 = 2$ and $\gamma^1 = 0$, the critical value for x_1^1/X^1 is 0.57. That is to say, when there are only two domestic firms which export their entire output and there are no other firms in the world, monopoly by the more efficient firm is always better than duopoly. This result can be extended to the case where the domestic country has more than two firms, as proved below.

Corollary *When a number of only domestic oligopolists compete for a foreign market and there is no domestic demand, all the firms except the most efficient one should be eliminated.*

Proof. Since there are N firms in the market, the maximum market share of the least efficient firm is $1/N$. Thus, if we can show that the critical share of x_1^1/X^1 is more than $1/N$ for any $N \geq 2$, the conclusion should follow. Since $\gamma^1 = 0$, $e^1 = X^1$, and $N = n^1$, from proposition 4.5 the critical share of x_1^1/X^1 is $2N/((N+1)^2 - N)$. This critical share is more than $1/N$ if and only if $N^2 > N + 1$ and the latter condition is satisfied for all $N \geq 2$.   □

---

[8] Needless to say, the denominator on the right-hand side of the inequality in proposition 4.5 is positive since $N \geq n^1$ and $0 \leq \gamma^1 \leq 1$.

4.5   The presence of foreign ownership

In the preceding sections we assumed all the firms located in one country to be domestically owned and thus all foreign commodities to be supplied only through trade. In this section we relax that assumption and generalize propositions 4.1, 4.2 and 4.3. We now assume that country j owns n^j firms and that these firms can be located in any of the m countries.[9] Theorem 1 can almost be repeated with one important difference: the definition of exports e^j now has to be modified.

Theorem 2

$$dW^j = (-f') \left(\sum_{i=1}^{n^j} x_i^j dx_i^j - \tilde{e}^j dD \right) \quad (for \ j = 2, \ldots, m)$$

(4.18)

$$and \quad dW^1 = (-f') \left(\sum_{i=1}^{n^1} x_i^1 dx_i^1 - \tilde{e}^1 dD \right) - x_1^1 dc_1^1,$$

(4.19)

where $\tilde{e}^j$ is the total production of firms owned by country j minus total demand in country j, i.e.,

$$\tilde{e}^j = \sum_{i=1}^{n^j} x_i^j - D^j.$$

(4.20)

In view of the similarity between theorems 1 and 2, propositions 4.1, 4.2 and 4.3 can be replicated after taking into account the new definitions of 'exports' and 'imports'.

Proposition 4.6 *An increase in the marginal costs of, or elimination of, a minor firm in a country unambiguously benefits the country if its global production is larger than the domestic demand for the commodity. The same result also holds even when the global production is smaller than the domestic demand provided the difference between the two quantities is sufficiently small. Such a change or elimination harms the country if its total domestic production is much smaller than its demand. If there is only one significant producer in a country and its marginal costs increase, the country is unambiguously worse off.*

Proposition 4.7 *If all the firms owned by a country are identical, an increase in the marginal costs of one of the firms unambiguously harms the country.*

[9] Even a small policy change may affect the location of a firm and thus generate a discrete effect on the market structure, as Hortsmann and Markusen (1992) show. However, the present chapter ignores this possibility and assumes that the international location of firms is not affected by policy changes.

Proposition 4.8 *An increase in the marginal costs of, or elimination of, a firm in one country benefits its trading partners whose global production exceeds domestic demand, and harms those whose global production is much smaller than domestic demand. These properties are valid irrespective of whether the firm is minor, major or identical to all the other firms owned by the country.*

The above propositions speak for themselves. Here we shall explain, with the help of an example, how the presence of foreign ownership may change the policy options facing a country. The USA is possibly a net importer of automobiles in the conventional sense of the term. Thus, according to proposition 4.1, eliminating a minor firm in the USA may not improve its welfare. Moreover, proposition 4.3 suggests that similar policies pursued by Japan or Europe may be detrimental to the welfare of the USA. However, since the foreign subsidiaries of Ford and General Motors have significant stakes in markets abroad, the USA may be a net exporter of automobiles in the sense that the global production by US owned firms exceeds its domestic consumption of automobiles. Thus, from proposition 4.8, the USA may not have any reason to complain if Japan or Europe adopts industrial policies of the type discussed above. Moreover, proposition 4.6 suggests that the USA itself should pursue such policies to its benefit. Our results here are in line with the findings by Dick (1993) who found that many of the standard results in the strategic trade policy literature do not go through in the presence of cross-ownership of firms.

4.6   Production subsidies

The preceding sections analysed the welfare effects of a small exogenous change in the marginal costs of a firm. As we have seen, these comparative static exercises can be used to analyse the welfare implications of entry–exit policies. However, changes in the marginal costs have no policy relevance. This section analyses the welfare effects of changes in the marginal costs of a firm induced by tax/subsidy policies. In particular, it examines the effect of introducing a production tax or subsidy on a firm – say firm 1 in country 1 – on the welfare levels of all the countries.

To be more specific, we consider a small change in s_1^1 when the initial values of all the subsidies are zero ($s_i^j = 0$ for all i and j) and all the firms in a country are domestically owned. In this case, from the equations in section 4.2 the main theorem is obtained.[10]

---

[10] The terms involving ds_i^j do not explicitly appear in (4.21). Implicitly, however, changes in s_i^j's affect welfare through changes in x_i^j's and D represented by dx_i^j's and dD.

Theorem 3

$$dW^j = (-f') \left(\sum_{i=1}^{n^j} x_i^j \, dx_i^j - e^j \, dD \right) \qquad (\text{for } j = 1, \ldots, m).$$

(4.21)

Theorem 3 is once again very similar to theorem 1. Moreover, in appendix A we have derived the expressions for dx_i^j / ds_1^1 and dD/ds_1^1 (see (A.4.5) in appendix A). Comparing (A.4.2) and (A.4.3) with (A.4.5), we find that an increase in c_1^1 has the same effect on x_1^1 and D as a decrease in s_1^1. Thus, propositions 4.1, 4.2 and 4.3 of section 4.3 can be replicated with minor modifications.

Proposition 4.9 *A production tax on a minor firm in a country unambiguously benefits the country if it is an exporter (or even a minor importer) of the commodity, and harms the country if its total domestic production is much smaller than its demand. If there is only one significant producer in a country and it is taxed, the country is unambiguously worse off.*

Proposition 4.10 *If all the firms in a country are identical, taxing the production of one of the firms unambiguously harms the country.*

Proposition 4.11 *A production tax on a firm in a country benefits other countries if they are exporters (or even minor importers), and harms them if in those countries domestic production is much smaller than domestic demand. These properties are valid irrespective of whether the firm is minor, major or identical to all the other firms in the country.*

The statements of the above propositions are self-explanatory and we shall not dwell on them. However, it is worth noting how they relate to the literature. The final part of proposition 4.9 generalizes a result in Brander and Spencer (1985). In a model of international duopoly, i.e., one firm in each of two countries, where the two firms compete for a market in a third country, they prove that it is advantageous for each country to subsidize its firm. However, the first part of proposition 4.9 casts a shadow on this result by showing that in the presence of more than one firm in a country a production tax on a minor firm makes the country better off.

Dixit (1984) also shows that it may be optimal for a country to tax domestic production. However, he assumes that all domestic firms are symmetric and that a uniform tax/subsidy rate is applied to all domestic firms. The possibility of taxing domestic firms arises because of the asymmetry between domestic and foreign firms. In the present analysis, in contrast, the asymmetry among domestic firms causes a discriminatory production tax to benefit the home country.

4.7 Conclusion

Although the literature on international oligopoly is large, hitherto very little work has been done on the welfare effect of an entry–exit policy when oligopolists within a country have different levels of marginal costs. In the literature this issue has been dealt with only within a closed-economy framework. This is particularly surprising because this type of industrial policy is outside the realm of GATT regulations and a country can use this policy for strategic gains.

This chapter has attempted to fill this void in the literature by considering a fairly general model of an international oligopoly. In this process we have generalized many of the results that one comes across in the literature, brought together various strands in the literature, and also proved many new ones. In particular, trade patterns (whether a country exports or imports) have been shown to be crucial in the derivation of the welfare effects of a discriminatory entry–exit policy and of a production tax. For example, eliminating a minor firm in a country benefits the country if it is a net exporter (or even a minor importer) of the oligopoly commodity. If a country is a significant importer, on the contrary, eliminating a firm in the country harms it and benefits its trading partners if they are exporters of the commodity.

Appendix A

In this appendix we derive the effect of changes in c_1^1 (or s_1^1) on D and x_i^j's. We assume that $s_i^j = 0$ and work out the effects of changes in c_1^1. The analysis with respect to s_1^1 is similar and only the results will be given at the end.

Total differentiation of (4.4) generates

$$\left(f' + x_i^j f''\right)dD + f'dx_i^j = dc_i^j - ds_i^j. \qquad (A.4.1)$$

Since we first ignore s_i^j's, $ds_i^j = 0$ for all i and j. Also, we consider the case where $dc_i^j = 0$ for all i and j except for $i = j = 1$. Therefore, summing over the above equations for all i's and j's and making use of (4.3) gives

$$\frac{dD}{dc_1^1} = \frac{1}{(N+1)f' + f''D}, \qquad (A.4.2)$$

whence substituting (A.4.1) into (A.4.2) gives

$$\frac{dx_i^j}{dc_1^1} = \begin{cases} \dfrac{Nf'+(D-x_1^1)f''}{f'((N+1)f'+Df'')} & \text{if } i=j=1 \\[3mm] -\dfrac{f'+x_i^j f''}{f'((N+1)f'+Df'')} & \text{otherwise} \end{cases}$$

where $\quad N = \displaystyle\sum_{j=1}^{m} n^j.$ (A.4.3)

Because of assumption 4.1, it is clear from the above two equations that

$$\frac{dx_i^j}{dc_1^1} \begin{cases} <0 & \text{if } i=j=1 \\[2mm] >0 & \text{otherwise} \end{cases}$$

and $\quad \dfrac{dD}{dc_1^1} < 0,$ (A.4.4)

Similarly, from (A.4.1),

$$\frac{dx_i^j}{ds_1^1} = \begin{cases} -\dfrac{Nf'+(D-x_1^1)f''}{f'((N+1)f'+Df'')} > 0 & \text{if } i=j=1 \\[3mm] \dfrac{f'+x_i^j f''}{f'((N+1)f'+Df'')} < 0 & \text{otherwise} \end{cases}$$

and $\quad \dfrac{dD}{ds_1^1} = -\dfrac{1}{(N+1)f'+f''D} > 0.$ (A.4.5)

Appendix B

In this appendix we provide the proofs of propositions 4.1–4.3.

Proof of proposition 4.1: For the first part of the proposition, without loss of generality, we assume that the minor firm whose marginal cost rises is firm 1 in country 1, i.e., $x_1^1 \simeq 0$ and $dc_1^1 > 0$. From (4.8) and (4.10), it is clear that the welfare of country 1 unambiguously increases with c_1^1 if e^1 is either (1) positive or (2) negative but its absolute value is not very large. Furthermore, if the domestic production of the country is much smaller than its demand, then $e^1 \ll 0$ and $x_i^1/e^1 \simeq 0$ for all i. Therefore, from (4.8) and (4.10), an increase in c_1^1 lowers country 1's welfare. Note that the above results continue to hold as the marginal cost rises and eventually the firm is eliminated from the market.

For the second part, firm 1 in country 1 is assumed to be a major firm domestically, i.e., $x_k^1 \simeq 0$ for $k \neq 1$ and $dc_1^1 > 0$. In this case, totally differentiating (4.4) in which s_i^j is ignored and applying the result to equation (4.8), we get

$$\frac{1}{x_1^1} dW^1 = -f'' x_1^1 dD - 2f' dx_1^1 - \frac{f' D^1 dD}{x_1^1} \qquad (B.4.1)$$

$$= -(2f' + x_1^1 f'') dx_1^1 - f'' x_1^1 d(D - x_1^1) - \frac{f' D^1 dD}{x_1^1}. \qquad (B.4.2)$$

Since $f' < 0$, from (4.10) and (B.4.1) it follows that $dW^1/dc_1^1 < 0$ if $f'' \leq 0$. Since $D = \sum_{i,j} x_i^j$, using assumption 4.1, (4.10), and (B.4.2), we obtain $dW^1/dc_1^1 < 0$ if $f'' \geq 0$. Therefore, dW^1/dc_1^1 is negative irrespective of the sign of f''. □

Proof of proposition 4.2: From (4.10), an increase in c_1^1 decreases D and hence increases p, which reduces consumers' surplus. Next we shall show that it also reduces producers' surplus in country 1. To see this, totally differentiating (4.2) and applying (4.4) to the result, we obtain

$$d\left(\sum_{i=1}^{n^1} \pi_i^1\right) = f' \sum_{i=1}^{n^1} n^1 x_i^1 dD - f' \sum_{i=1}^{n^1} n^1 (x_i^1 dx_i^1) - x_1^1 dc_1^1. \qquad (B.4.3)$$

Using (A.4.2), (A.4.3) and the symmetry, i.e., $x_i^1 = x_1^1$ for all i, equation (B.4.3) can be written as

$$\frac{d\left(\sum_{i=1}^{n^1} \pi_i^1\right)}{dc_1^1}$$
$$= \frac{x_1^1 \{(n^1 x_1^1 - 2D)(2f' + Df'') + 2f'(D(n^1 + 1 - N) - n^1 x_1^1)\}}{D((N+1)f' + Df'')}, \qquad (B.4.4)$$

where $N = \sum_{j=1}^{m} n^j$. From assumption 4.1 and the above equation, we find

$$\frac{d\left(\sum_{i=1}^{n^1} \pi_i^1\right)}{dc_1^1} < 0.$$

Thus both consumers' and producers' surpluses go down as a result of an increase in the marginal cost of one of the firms. □

Proof of proposition 4.3: From (4.7) and (4.10), it is clear that an increase in c_1^1 raises the welfare of country j ($j \neq 1$) if e^j is either (1) positive or (2) negative but its absolute value is not very large. If production is much smaller than demand in country j ($j \neq 1$), then $x_i^j / e^j \simeq 0$ for all i and $e^j \ll 0$, and hence from (4.7) and (4.10) an increase in c_1^j makes country j worse off. Note that both of these properties are valid no matter how large the output of the firm whose marginal cost increases is.   □

Appendix C

This appendix obtains the closed-form solution for some of the variables under linear demand and no subsidy to any firm ($s_i^j = 0$ for all i and j).

By substituting (4.15) into (4.4) one obtains

$$\alpha - \beta D = c_i^j + \beta x_i^j. \tag{C.4.1}$$

Now summing (C.4.1) over all i's and j's and making use of (4.3), the solution for D is

$$D = \frac{N\alpha - \sum_{j=1}^{m} \sum_{i=1}^{n^j} c_i^j}{\beta(N+1)}. \tag{C.4.2}$$

The solutions for x_i^j's are obtained by substituting the solution for D (equation (C.4.2)) into (C.4.1). They are

$$(N+1)\beta x_i^j = \alpha - (N+1)c_i^j + \sum_{j=1}^{m} \sum_{i=1}^{n^j} c_i^j. \tag{C.4.3}$$

From (4.2), (4.4) and (4.15), we have

$$\pi_i^1 = \beta \left(x_i^1\right)^2. \tag{C.4.4}$$

Since $D^1 = \gamma^1 D$ and the inverse demand function for country 1 is

$$p = \alpha - \frac{\beta}{\gamma^1} D^1,$$

consumers' surplus in country 1 is

$$CS^1 = \frac{\gamma^1 \beta D^2}{2}. \tag{C.4.5}$$

Applying (C.4.4) and (C.4.5) to (4.5) leads to

$$W^1\left(x_i^1\right) = \beta \sum_{i=1}^{n^1} \left(x_i^1\right)^2 + \frac{\gamma^1 \beta D^2}{2}. \tag{C.4.6}$$

The substitution of (C.4.2) and (C.4.3) into (C.4.6) and some manipulations yield

$$W^1(x_1^1) = \theta + \beta(x_1^1)^2 \left(1 + \frac{2(n^1 - 1) + \gamma^1}{2N^2} \right) + \frac{x_1^1}{N} \left(\alpha\gamma^1 + 2\sum_{i=2}^{n^1} c_i^1 \right.$$
$$\left. - \frac{(2(n^1 - 1) + \gamma^1)\left(\alpha + \sum_{j=1}^{m} \sum_{i=1}^{n^j} c_i^j - c_1^1\right)}{N} \right). \quad \text{(C.4.7)}$$

Summing (C.4.3) over i's for $j = 1$ and making use of (4.12) gives

$$(N + 1)\beta X^1 = n^1\alpha - \sum_{i=1}^{n^1} c_i^1 + n^1 \sum_{j=1}^{m} \sum_{i=1}^{n^j} c_i^j. \quad \text{(C.4.8)}$$

Finally, substituting $\sum_{j=1}^{m} \sum_{i=1}^{n^j} c_i^j$ into (C.4.7) with the help of (C.4.8), we obtain (4.16) in the text.

5 Trade policy when producers and sellers differ

5.1 Introduction

The literature on the nature and the structure of optimal tariffs is an old one in the theory of international trade. There are many arguments for the imposition of tariffs, the most well-known argument being the monopoly power in trade – the terms of trade argument (see Bhagwati and Ramaswamy, 1963): since a large country can affect the international terms of trade by imposing tariffs, it can use tariffs to maximize its own welfare.[1] There are other reasons, such as monopoly power in production (Katrak, 1977), unalterable domestic distortions,[2] the infant industry argument (see Corden, 1974, ch. 9), etc., for a country to impose tariffs in order to raise its welfare.

The above literature ignores one important aspect of real life, viz., the fact that often producers and sellers of a commodity are different entities. For example, Toyota cars are most often sold abroad by dealers that are nationals of the country where the cars are sold. Another example is the clothing industry where items are usually sold by big stores under their own brand names (e.g., St. Michael for Marks and Spencer) but are often produced not by the stores but by other domestic and/or foreign producers.

In deciding on the level of the optimal tariff on a commodity under this circumstance, the importing country clearly has to take into account its effect on the domestic sellers' profits. Can this new consideration change the sign of optimal tariffs? This is one of the questions that the present chapter addresses itself to.[3]

---

[1] The fact that a tariff can affect the international terms of trade was perhaps first recognized by Colonel Robert Torrens in the middle of the nineteenth century (see Viner, 1937, pp. 298–9). Subsequently, this issue has been subject to rigorous analyses (see, for example, Baldwin, 1960; Bhagwati and Johnson, 1961; and Jones, 1974); Metzler, 1949. The question of optimal tariffs in the presence of retaliation from the trading partners has been analysed by Johnson (1954–5) and Scitovsky (1949) among others.

[2] See Bhagwati (1971) for a generalized analysis of this subject.

[3] In the literature it is recognized that under certain circumstances the sign of optimal tariffs could be negative. Kemp (1967) and Riley (1970) have found that when there are multiple equilibria due to externalities, etc., optimal tariffs can be negative.

Once one distinguishes between producers and sellers, the nature of the oligopolistic relationship between the two groups also plays an important role in deriving the welfare implication of tariffs. In the two examples given above, it should be clear that the relationship between Toyota and its dealers in importing countries is fundamentally different from the relationship between Marks and Spencer and the firms which produce garments for it. In some cases producers take the leadership position and in others the followership position. Does the sign of the optimal tariff depend crucially on who the leader is? This is another question that this chapter attempts to answer. We analyse the properties of optimal tariffs under a number of alternative market structures.

In what follows we first describe the basic model in section 5.2, which has two subsections. In subsection 5.2.1 we describe a model in which a price-taking foreign producer exports its product to a dealer in the home country who in turn sells it in the domestic market. The monopoly seller is the leader in this model. By contrast, the seller is the follower in the model of subsection 5.2.2 and the commodity is produced by a foreign monopolist who is the leader in the vertical relationship between the producer and the seller.[4] The properties of optimal tariffs in these two cases are analysed in the two subsections of section 5.3.

Section 5.4 extends the basic model to allow for multiple producers and/or sellers with various patterns of oligopolistic interdependence between producers and/or sellers. Specifically, the following three alternative scenarios are considered. First, in subsection 5.4.1, we consider the case where a single domestic seller takes the leadership position over foreign and domestic producers. In the second and third scenarios we treat the case of a Cournot duopoly between two domestic sellers: one specific to a domestic producer and the other to a foreign producer. More specifically, in the second scenario (subsection 5.4.2) the sellers take the leadership position over each seller-specific producer in setting prices, whereas in the third (subsection 5.4.3) the producers are leaders. Some concluding remarks are made in section 5.5.

---

[4] In any of the models developed in this chapter where the strategic variable is quantity, we can appeal to the famous Kreps and Scheinkman (1983) result that a Cournot outcome holds for capacity-constrained price games. In the models where the strategic variable is price, we have to assume that price contracts are legally binding. Once an agent reneges on its commitment, it may also do so any number of times; and one has to draw a line somewhere. We, like most people, have drawn a line at the very first stage and have assumed a primitive restraint, namely that no one breaks a contract. Tirole (1988, pp. 170–1) in his discussion on this subject is very relaxed about such an assumption. We have simply considered a few seemingly realistic vertical market structures, and putting a game theoretic superstructure to our models will not add any new insight to the present analysis.

5.2   The benchmark model

We consider a single-commodity partial-equilibrium model with two countries: the home country and the foreign country. In this benchmark case we model a simple vertical relationship between a monopolist seller in the home country and the producer (or producers) of the commodity in a foreign country. The case with multiple sellers and/or oligopolistic producers will be taken up in section 5.4.

The inverse demand function for the commodity in the home country is given by

$$p = f(D), \quad f' < 0, \tag{5.1}$$

where p and D are respectively the domestic price and demand of the commodity. When the home country imposes *ad-valorem* tariff t on the imports of the commodity, the profit of the (domestic) seller and that of the (foreign) producer are written respectively as

$$\pi_s = (f(D) - (1 + t)q)D, \tag{5.2}$$
$$\pi_f = qD - c(D), \tag{5.3}$$

where $c(\cdot)$ is the cost function of the producer and q is the international price of the commodity.

The welfare of the home country, W_h, is the sum of consumers' surplus, CS_h, the seller's profits, π_s, and the government's tariff revenue, tqD, i.e.,

$$W_h = CS_h + \pi_s + tqD = CS_h + (f(D) - q)D. \tag{5.4}$$

It can easily be proved that

$$dCS_h = -Ddp = -Df'dD. \tag{5.5}$$

We shall complete the description of the basic model by presenting the profit maximization conditions for the producer and the seller. This will be done under two alternative assumptions on the relationship between the producer and the seller. In the first we assume the seller to be the leader and the producer the follower. In the second the relationship is the other way round.[5]

---

[5] We do not analyse what determines who the leader is, rather take this choice as exogenous. An interesting extension would be to endogenize the question of leadership and relate it to some variables like market shares or relative costs as in Ono (1978, 1982). However, in our framework this would introduce enormous difficulties and therefore we have decided to treat the leadership issue in an exogenous fashion.

5.2.1   The case of leadership by the seller

When the seller acts as a leader, the producer takes international price q as given,[6] and hence its profit maximization condition is simply

$$q = c'(D). \tag{5.6}$$

Since the seller, who is the leader, maximizes (5.2) by taking into account the producer's reaction function (given by (5.6)), its profit maximization condition is given by

$$\frac{d\pi_s}{dD} = p - (1+t)c'(D) + (f'(D) - (1+t)c''(D))D = 0. \tag{5.7}$$

For the concavity of the profit function to hold, it is assumed that

Assumption 5.1

$$\Delta_s \equiv 2(f'(D) - (1+t)c''(D)) + D(f''(D) - (1+t)c'''(D)) < 0.$$

5.2.2   The case of leadership by the producer

In the alternative scenario there is only one foreign producer who is the leader and the seller is the follower. The seller maximizes profits by taking q as given. Thus, the maximizing condition is

$$f(D) + Df'(D) = (1+t)q,$$

from which the seller's reaction function is derived to be

$$q = q(D,t) = \frac{f(D) + Df'(D)}{1+t},$$

$$\text{with} \quad \frac{\partial q}{\partial D} \equiv q_D = \frac{Df''(D) + 2f'(D)}{1+t},$$

$$\text{and} \quad \frac{\partial q}{\partial t} \equiv q_t = -\frac{q}{1+t}. \tag{5.8}$$

The foreign producer maximizes π_f given in (5.3), taking into account the seller's reaction, as in (5.8), and thus yielding

$$Dq_D(D,t) + q(D,t) = c'(D). \tag{5.9}$$

Since the profit function of the producer is assumed to be concave, we must have

Assumption 5.2

$$\Delta_f \equiv q_{DD}D + 2q_D - c''(D) < 0.$$

This completes the description of the two cases of bilateral monopoly.

---

[6] Even if there are multiple producers in this case, the results do not change.

5.3   Optimal tariffs

In this section we shall obtain the signs of optimal tariffs under the two alternative producer–seller relationships described in the preceding section. We first consider the case where the seller is the leader.

5.3.1   The case of leadership by the seller

In this case, by totally differentiating (5.4) and making use of (5.2), (5.5) and (5.6), one gets

$$dW_h = \{p - c'(D) - Dc''(D)\}dD. \tag{5.10}$$

From (5.10) it is clear that optimal tariff t^* must satisfy

$$f(D) = c'(D) + Dc''(D). \tag{5.11}$$

Using (5.7) and (5.11) we obtain t^*:

$$t^* = \frac{Df'(D)}{p},$$

which is negative because of (5.1). Formally,

Proposition 5.1 *If the seller is the leader, the optimal tariff is unambiguously negative.*

Note that this result is in sharp contrast to the conventional optimal tariff theory in a competitive setting. In the present case the domestic seller is the leader and its monopoly power causes distortion, whereas the foreign producer takes the international price to be given and therefore behaves competitively. Import subsidies increase the supply of the seller by lowering its unit cost, and thereby reduce the distortion. In fact, differentiating (5.7) and using assumption 5.1 and (5.11) yield

$$\frac{dD}{dt} = \frac{c'(D) + Dc''(D)}{\Delta_s} < 0, \quad \frac{dp}{dt} > 0 \quad \text{when } t = t^*, \tag{5.12}$$

which implies that a decrease in t raises D and reduces p. If it were not for this distortion, the optimal tariff would definitely be positive, as is well known, since it would enable the importing country to exercise monopoly power in trade. Proposition 5.1 shows that the former effect dominates the latter and thus import subsidies make the home country better off.

The above mechanism works in a clear-cut fashion in the special case of constant marginal costs ($c'' = 0$). In this case, $p = c' = q$, which implies that the equilibrium price and quantity at the optimum equals the competitive equilibrium values. The reason is that if the foreign producer faces constant marginal costs (i.e., if the supply function is perfectly elastic), then there is no rationale for a positive tariff; the negative optimal tariff in this case only corrects for the monopolistic power of the domestic seller.

5.3.2   The case of leadership by the producer

Having established the sign of the optimal tariff in the case where the seller is the leader, we now turn to the case where the producer is the leader. Here we consider two cases; linear demand and demand with constant price elasticity. First, we deal with the case of linear demand:

$$p = \alpha - \beta D. \tag{5.13}$$

Applying (5.13) into (5.4), (5.5), (5.8) and (5.9) gives

$$\left. \frac{dW_h}{dt} \right|_{t=0} = -\frac{D[\alpha\beta + 4\beta^2 D + \{c'(D) + 2\beta D\}c''(D)]}{\Delta_f},$$

which, because of assumption 5.2, is positive unless the cost function is too concave. Thus, in the case of a linear demand function, the optimal tariff is positive unless the cost function is too concave.

Second, when the demand function is of the constant elasticity type, i.e., when $(dD/dp) \cdot (p/D) = (p/(Df'(D))) = -\epsilon$ and $\epsilon > 1$,

$$\left. \frac{dW_h}{dt} \right|_{t=0} = -\frac{(\epsilon - 1)p\{\epsilon c''(D) + (\epsilon - 1)f'(D)\}}{(\epsilon)^2 D\Delta_f}.$$

From the above equation it is evident that

$$\left. \frac{dW_h}{dt} \right|_{t=0} \gtreqless 0 \iff \{f'(D) + c''(D)\}\epsilon - f'(D) \gtreqless 0.$$

Thus, the optimal tariff can be either positive or negative under a constant elasticity demand function and it would be negative if the cost function is not very convex.

The above results can formally be stated as

Proposition 5.2 *When the foreign producer is the leader, the optimal tariff can be either positive or negative. When the demand function is linear, for example, the optimal tariff is positive if the cost function is not too concave. When the demand function is of the constant elasticity type, the optimal tariff is negative if and only if* $c''(D) < -(\epsilon - 1)f'/\epsilon.$

Unlike the previous case, there are two monopoly distortions: one caused by the domestic seller's monopoly power over the domestic market (which also exists in the previous case) and the other by the foreign producer's leadership over the domestic seller. Accordingly, there are two effects of tariffs on welfare: (1) the monopoly effect due to the monopoly power of the seller, and (2) the monopoly effect due to the monopoly power of the foreign producer. The first effect calls for an import subsidy, as mentioned in the previous case. The second effect calls for an import tariff since it reduces the derived demand of the product and thus lowers the international price, generating a profit-shifting effect from the foreign producer. Clearly, the more concave the demand function is, the more effective would be the profit-shifting effect. Since a linear demand function is more concave than a constant elasticity one, the second effect is stronger under the former than under the latter. Thus, we obtain proposition 5.2.

The model of this subsection can be viewed as an extension of the model due to Katrak (1977) and of the basic model in Brander and Spencer (1984) in which a single foreign producer sells a commodity directly to the domestic consumers.

5.4   Various oligopolistic situations

In the preceding sections we set up and analysed a model of bilateral monopoly with a domestic seller and a foreign producer. In this section we shall relax these assumptions by considering multiple sellers or producers and adding rivalry among sellers or producers to the model of the previous section. There are three extensions of it. In the first extension a single domestic seller purchases the commodity from a foreign producer as well as a domestic one. The seller takes the leadership position over the two producers in this case. In the second and third extensions we consider two competing domestic sellers: one specific to a foreign producer and the other to a domestic producer. Whereas in the second extension each seller takes the leadership position over each specific producer, in the third extension the producers are leaders.[7]

5.4.1   The case of leadership by a monopolist seller

We first consider the case where a single domestic seller takes the leadership position over a foreign and a domestic producer. The foreign and

---

[7] In the present context, we shall continue to obtain properties of optimal tariffs. However, in the presence of domestic producers a tariff may not be the first best-policy instrument. In fact, in the presence of domestic producers a combination of a production subsidy to the domestic producers and a sales tax would dominate a tariff. However, in order to be able to compare the results with those of the previous section, we consider the second-best policy of an import tariff.

domestic producers are respectively assumed to have cost functions $c_f(x_f)$ and $c_d(x_d)$ where x_f and x_d denote the output of the respective producers.

Given international price q and tariff t, the foreign producer faces price q whereas the domestic producer faces $(1+t)q$. Therefore, the two producers have the following profit functions respectively.

$$\pi_f = qx_f - c_f(x_f),$$
$$\pi_d = (1+t)qx_d - c_d(x_d). \tag{5.14}$$

The profit maximization conditions are

$$q = c_f'(x_f),$$
$$(1+t)q = c_d'(x_d). \tag{5.15}$$

The seller maximizes its profits given by

$$\pi_s = [f(D) - (1+t)q]D, \tag{5.16}$$

taking into account the reactions of the producers, given by (5.15). D in the above equation represents the total output by the two producers, i.e.,

$$D = x_f + x_d. \tag{5.17}$$

From (5.15)–(5.17) international price q is expressed as a function of D and t:

$$q = q(D, t), \tag{5.18}$$

where

$$q_D = \frac{c_f'' c_d''}{(1+t)c_f'' + c_d''},$$

$$q_t = -\frac{q c_f''}{(1+t)c_f'' + c_d''},$$

$$q_{D_t}(D, t) = -\frac{(c_f'')^2 c_d''}{\{(1+t)c_f'' + c_d''\}^2}.$$

Given tariff t, the seller maximizes (5.16) subject to (5.18), yielding

$$f(D) + Df'(D) = (1+t)\{q + Dq_D(D, t)\}. \tag{5.19}$$

The concavity of the profit function requires

Assumption 5.3

$$\Delta'_s \equiv 2f'(D) + Df''(D) - (1 + t)\{2q_D(D, t) + q_{DD}(D, t)D\} < 0.$$

Finally, the welfare of the home country in this case is

$$W_h = CS_h + \pi_d + \pi_s + tqx_f, \tag{5.20}$$

where CS_h satisfies (5.5) and π_d and π_s are given in (5.14) and (5.16) respectively.

Using the above equations we obtain the optimal tariff. The total differentiation of (5.19) gives

$$\frac{dD}{dt} = \frac{c''_d\{Dc''_f c''_d + (1 + t)qc''_f + qc''_d\}}{\Delta'_s\{(1 + t)c''_f + c''_d\}^2}. \tag{5.21}$$

Totally differentiating (5.20) and using (5.14), (5.15)–(5.17) and (5.19) yield

$$dW_h = \left[-Df'(D) + \left\{ (1 + t)x_d + tx_f + \frac{tq}{c''_f} \right\} q_D(D, t) \right] dD$$
$$+ \frac{tq q_t(D, t)}{c''_f} dt.$$

From the above equation tariff t^* is

$$t^* = -\frac{\{-Df'(D) + x_d q_D(D, t)\}\frac{dD}{dt}}{\left\{ Dq_D(D, t) + \frac{qq_D(D,t)}{c''_f} \right\}\frac{dD}{dt} + \frac{qq_t(D,t)}{c''_f}}.$$

Clearly, in view of (5.1), (5.18) and (5.21), as long as the cost functions are convex,

$$t^* < 0.$$

Formally, the above result is stated as follows:

Proposition 5.3 *If the seller is the leader and the cost functions are convex, the optimal tariff is negative even in the presence of a domestic producer that competes with a foreign producer.*

In addition to the two effects explained just below proposition 5.1, viz., the domestic seller's monopoly distortion and the importing country's monopoly power in trade, here we have another effect of a tariff, which is on the domestic producer's profits. Since the domestic producer is a follower and produces up to the point where the domestic price equals the marginal cost, this effect is small enough to be dominated by the effect due to the monopoly power of the seller. Thus, the sign of the optimal tariff remains negative as in proposition 5.1.

This subsection assumes that there are two producers, one domestic and one foreign. However, the results of this subsection can directly be applied to the case of multiple domestic and foreign producers since the producers are followers and hence behave competitively.

5.4.2 Leadership by duopolist sellers with seller-specific producers

Next we assume that there are two domestic sellers: one of them purchases the commodity exclusively from a domestic producer whereas the other from a foreign producer. The sellers take the leadership position over the producers. In the domestic market the two sellers compete with each other à la Cournot.[8]

The profits of the two producers and the first-order profit-maximizing conditions thereof are

$$\pi_d^p = q_d x_d - c_d(x_d),$$
$$\pi_f^p = q_f x_f - c_f(x_f), \tag{5.22}$$
$$q_d = c_d'(x_d) \quad \text{and} \quad q_f = c_f'(x_f).$$

From (5.22) the profits for the sellers are written as

$$\pi_d^s = [f(D) - q_d]x_d = [f(x_d + x_f) - c_d'(x_d)]x_d,$$
$$\pi_f^s = [f(D) - (1+t)q_f]x_f = [f(x_d + x_f) - (1+t)c_f'(x_f)]x_f. \tag{5.23}$$

Assuming Cournot conjectures, the first-order profit-maximizing conditions are

$$\frac{\partial \pi_d^s}{\partial x_d} = [f'(D) - c_d''(x_d)]x_d + p - c_d'(x_d) = 0,$$

$$\frac{\partial \pi_f^s}{\partial x_f} = [f'(D) - (1+t)c_f''(x_f)]x_f + p - (1+t)c_f'(x_f) = 0. \tag{5.24}$$

---

[8] Even if there are multiple producers specific to a seller, the results would not change.

Finally, from (5.22) and (5.23), the welfare of the home country is

$$W_h = CS_h + \pi_d^p + \pi_d^s + \pi_f^s + tq_f x_f$$
$$= CS_h + pD - c_d(x_d) - c_f'(x_f)x_f. \qquad (5.25)$$

Totally differentiating the two equations in (5.24), we obtain

$$(f''x_d + f')dx_f + \pi_{d,xx}^s dx_d = 0,$$
$$(f''x_f + f')dx_d + \pi_{f,xx}^s dx_f = (c_f' + x_f c_f'')dt,$$

where $\pi_{i,xx}^s = \partial^2 \pi_i^s / \partial x_i^2$ for $i = d, f$, and thus

$$\frac{dx_d}{dt} = \frac{(f''x_d + f')(c_f' + x_f c_f'')}{\Gamma},$$
$$\frac{dx_f}{dt} = -\frac{\pi_{d,xx}^s(c_f' + x_f c_f'')}{\Gamma}, \qquad (5.26)$$

where

$$\Gamma = (f''x_f + f')(f''x_d + f') - \pi_{d,xx}^s \pi_{f,xx}^s.$$

The stability of the equilibrium requires Γ to be negative. The profit functions of the sellers are assumed to be concave. Also, we assume the two sellers to be strategic substitutes. All of these are formally stated as

Assumption 5.4

$\Gamma < 0$, $\pi_{i,xx}^s < 0$ ($i = d, f$) and $f'(D) + xf''(D) < 0$ for all $D \geq x > 0$.

Finally, totally differentiating (5.25) and using (5.5), (5.24) and (5.26), we obtain

$$\left.\frac{dW_h}{dt}\right|_{t=0} = \frac{c_f' + x_f c_f''}{\Gamma}[(-f' + c_d'')(f' + f''x_f)x_d + f'x_f\pi_{d,xx}^s]. \qquad (5.27)$$

From assumption 5.4, and (5.27), as long as the cost functions are not too concave,

$$t^* > 0 \quad \text{if} \quad x_d \gg x_f,$$
$$\text{and} \quad t^* < 0 \quad \text{if} \quad x_f \gg x_d.$$

The above result can formally be stated as

Proposition 5.4 *Suppose that two sellers, one specific to the domestic producer and the other specific to the foreign producer, take the leadership position over the producers. If the market share of the domestic product is sufficiently large (small), the optimal tariff is positive (negative) as long as the cost functions are not too concave.*

The present situation is somewhat similar to the ones in chapters 1 and 4 (see also Lahiri and Ono, 1988 and 1997) in which there are two domestic firms with cost differences. In that framework taxing the firm with a much lower market share benefits the country. In the present framework there are two sellers whose profits accrue to the domestic country, and their cost structures are determined by the efficiency levels of the respective producers. If the market share of the syndicate of the domestic seller and the foreign producer is much lower, applying the mechanisms of chapters 1 and 4 we find that harming the foreign syndicate with the help of a positive tariff benefits the country.

The above result may also be explained in a different way. As shown in subsection 5.3.1, the optimal tariff is negative when the seller is the leader and there are no domestic producers. We take this as the benchmark case in providing an intuition for the above result. In the presence of domestic production there is an additional effect which is the so-called profit-shifting effect à la Brander and Spencer (1985). This effect would entail subsidizing the domestic syndicate. When its market share is high, the profit-shifting effect would dominate the benchmark effect and the optimal policy is to impose a positive tariff.

As Dixit (1984) and Neary (1988) have noted, the sign of the optimal tariff may depend on the number of domestic firms. In the present case, as the number of domestic sellers increases, the marginal contribution of profits by the domestic syndicates would decrease. Therefore, the addition of an extra domestic syndicate would lower the likelihood of a positive optimal tariff. In particular, under free entry of domestic syndicates the same argument would apply.

5.4.3 Leadership by duopolist producers

In this subsection we consider the same market structure as in subsection 5.4.2 except that the producers are leaders. In this case, the profits of the sellers are given by

$$\pi_f^s = [f(x_f + x_d) - q_f(1 + t)]x_f,$$
$$\pi_d^s = [f(x_f + x_d) - q_d]x_d. \tag{5.28}$$

From these equations, the first order conditions are

$$f(x_f + x_d) - q_f(1 + t) + f'(x_f + x_d)x_f = 0,$$
$$f(x_f + x_d) - q_d + f'(x_f + x_d)x_d = 0. \tag{5.29}$$

From (5.29) the following reaction functions are obtained

$$x_f = x_f(q_d, \hat{q}_f),$$
$$x_d = x_d(q_d, \hat{q}_f), \tag{5.30}$$

where $\hat{q}_f = q_f(1 + t)$.

The profits of the two producers are given by

$$\pi_f^p = q_f x_f(q_d, \hat{q}_f) - c_f(x_f(q_d, \hat{q}_f)),$$
$$\pi_d^p = q_d x_d(q_d, \hat{q}_f) - c_d(x_d(q_d, \hat{q}_f)). \tag{5.31}$$

Each producer maximizes profits with respect to the price that it charges to the seller specific to itself, taking the price charged by the other producer as given. This gives us the two profit maximizing conditions:

$$(q_f - c_f')x_f^f(1 + t) + x_f = 0,$$
$$(q_d - c_d')x_d^d + x_d = 0, \tag{5.32}$$

where

$$x_f^f = \frac{\partial x_f}{\partial \hat{q}_f}, \quad x_d^d = \frac{\partial x_d}{\partial q_d}.$$

Finally, in view of (5.28) and (5.31), the home country's welfare is

$$W_h = \pi_d^s + \pi_d^p + \pi_f^s + CS_h + tq_f x_f = pD - q_f x_f - c_d + CS_h. \tag{5.33}$$

Totally differentiating (5.33) and using (5.29) and (5.32) we get

$$dW_h = (-f'x_f + tq_f)dx_f + \left(-f'x_d - \frac{x_d}{x_d^d}\right)dx_d - x_f dq_f. \tag{5.34}$$

By assuming the marginal costs to be constant and considering the cases of linear and constant elasticity demand, from (5.34) we shall show below that the sign of the optimal tariff can be either positive or negative, as was the case in subsection 5.3.2.

When the demand function is linear, see (5.13), equation (5.34) reduces to

$$3\beta \left.\frac{dW_h}{dt}\right|_{t=0} = \left(-\frac{14}{15}c_f' + \alpha + \frac{2}{5}c_d'\right)x_f + \frac{2}{9}c_f'x_d > 0, \tag{5.35}$$

whose derivation is shown in appendix D. Thus, from (5.35), the optimal tariff is positive.

When the price elasticity of demand is constant at ϵ and the domestic and the foreign producer have the same level of marginal costs, i.e., $c_f = c_d = c$, equation (5.34) is

$$\frac{\Omega\left(2 - \frac{1}{\epsilon}\right)}{(3\epsilon - 1)Dc} \frac{dW_h}{dt}\bigg|_{t=0} = \frac{25\epsilon^4 - 2\epsilon^3 - 33\epsilon^2 + 22\epsilon - 4}{\epsilon^3}, \qquad (5.36)$$

where $\Omega = B^2 - A^2,$

$$A = \left(6 - \epsilon - \frac{4}{\epsilon}\right)(3\epsilon - 1) + 3(1 - \epsilon)^2,$$

$$B = \left(\epsilon - \frac{2}{\epsilon}\right)(3\epsilon - 1) - 3\left(2 + \epsilon - \frac{1}{\epsilon}\right)(\epsilon - 1),$$

whose derivation is shown in appendix D. For the price to be positive ϵ has to be greater than $1/2$, and for the system to be stable Ω must be negative. Therefore, the coefficient of $(dW_h/dt)|_{t=0}$ on the left-hand side of (5.36) is negative. It can also be verified that the numerator on the right-hand side of (5.36) is minimized at $\epsilon = 1/2$ and the minimum value is positive. Thus,

$$\frac{dW_h}{dt}\bigg|_{t=0} < 0,$$

and hence the optimal tariff is negative.

The results of this subsection are summarized below.

Proposition 5.5 *Suppose that there are two sellers, one specific to the domestic producer and the other specific to the foreign producer, and that the producers take the leadership position over the sellers. In this case the optimal tariff can be either negative or positive. In particular, the optimal tariff is positive if the demand function is linear. If the demand function is of the constant elasticity type and the two producers have the same level of marginal costs, the optimal tariff is negative.*

The intuition for this result is somewhat similar to the one provided for proposition 5.2. In the presence of the foreign producer's monopoly power, an import tariff lowers the international price and shifts some of the profits from the foreign producer. It also raises the profits of the domestic seller and producer. However, an import tariff raises the domestic price, which harms domestic consumers. The rise in the domestic price caused by an import tariff is much bigger under a constant-elasticity demand function than under a linear demand function. Under a constant-elasticy demand function, the large harmful effect on consumers' surplus happens to dominate the positive profit-shifting effect of a tariff, and the optimal tariff is negative. The opposite is true for linear demand.

5.5   Conclusion

In real life most commodities are sold not by producers but rather by dealers or traders who are typically distinct from the producers. In the literature of international trade, however, this distinction is not made. In analysing optimal tariffs, *inter alia*, the adverse effect of protectionist policies on the profits of domestic sellers is not taken into account.

In this chapter we analysed the nature of optimal tariffs by distinguishing between producers and sellers. The relationship between producers and sellers can of course take a wide variety of forms. This chapter considered two types of relationship: (1) leadership by sellers, and (2) leadership by producers. For each of the two types of relationship, we also examined different market structures. In particular, we considered the following market structures: (1) no domestic producer and a domestic monopolist seller purchasing only from a foreign producer, (2) a domestic monopolist seller purchasing from both domestic and foreign producers, and (3) domestic duopolist sellers: one specific to a foreign producer and the other to a domestic producer.

In the various settings mentioned above, we found that if there is only one seller who takes the leadership position over a producer (or producers), the optimal policy would be to subsidise imports irrespective of whether or not there is competing domestic production. In the case of domestic duopolist sellers that take the leadership position over each specific (foreign or domestic) producer, the sign of the optimal tariff depends on the market share of the two sellers. Finally, when the foreign and domestic producers take the leadership position over each specific seller, the nature of the demand curve is an important determinant of the sign of the optimal tariff.

To conclude, both the distinction between producers and sellers and the nature of the relationship between the two groups have important implications for the nature of the optimal import tariff–subsidy policy. It can be either positive or negative.

Appendix D

In this appendix we provide the detailed derivations of equations (5.35) (the case of linear demand) and (5.36) (the case of constant elastic demand) in section 5.4.

LINEAR DEMAND

When the demand function is linear (see (5.13)), equation (5.30) reduces to

$$\beta x_f = \frac{1}{3}\alpha - \frac{2}{3}\hat{q}_f + \frac{1}{3}q_d, \tag{D.5.1}$$

$$\beta x_d = \frac{1}{3}\alpha - \frac{2}{3}q_d + \frac{1}{3}\hat{q}_f. \tag{D.5.2}$$

Moreover, from (5.32), we find

$$\hat{q}_f = \frac{5\alpha + 8c'_f(1+t) + 2c'_d}{15}, \tag{D.5.3}$$

$$q_d = \frac{5\alpha + 8c'_d + 2c'_f(1+t)}{15}. \tag{D.5.4}$$

Substituting (D.5.3) and (D.5.4) into (D.5.1) and (D.5.2), we obtain

$$\beta x_f = \frac{2}{9}\alpha - \frac{14}{45}c'_f(1+t) + \frac{4}{45}c'_d, \tag{D.5.5}$$

$$\beta x_d = \frac{2}{9}\alpha - \frac{14}{45}c'_d + \frac{4}{45}c'_f(1+t). \tag{D.5.6}$$

Applying (D.5.2), (D.5.3) and (D.5.5) to (5.34), we get

$$3\beta \left.\frac{dW_h}{dt}\right|_{t=0} = \left(-\frac{14}{15}c'_f + \alpha + \frac{2}{5}c'_d\right)x_f + \frac{2}{9}c'_f x_d, \tag{D.5.7}$$

which is equation (5.35) in the text. Since $-\frac{14}{15}c'_f + \alpha + \frac{2}{5}c'_d > \frac{2}{3}\alpha - \frac{14}{15}c'_f + \frac{4}{15}c'_d = 3\beta x_f > 0$, from (D.5.5) this value is positive. Therefore, the optimal tariff is positive.

CONSTANT ELASTICITY DEMAND FUNCTION

When the demand function is of the constant elasticity type and the absolute value of the price elasticity of demand is ϵ, equations (5.29) and (5.32) are

$$p - \hat{q}_f - \frac{ps_f}{\epsilon} = 0, \tag{D.5.8}$$

$$p - \hat{q}_d - \frac{ps_d}{\epsilon} = 0, \tag{D.5.9}$$

$$-\frac{(\hat{q}_f - c'_f)(1+t)((1+s_f)\epsilon - s_d)}{p\left(2 - \frac{1}{\epsilon}\right)} + s_f = 0, \tag{D.5.10}$$

$$-\frac{(q_d - c'_d)((1+s_d)\epsilon - s_f)}{p\left(2 - \frac{1}{\epsilon}\right)} + s_d = 0. \tag{D.5.11}$$

where $s_i = x_i/D$, $i = d, f$, and hence $s_d + s_f = 1$. From (D.5.8) and (D.5.9), we find

$$p = \frac{\hat{q}_f + q_d}{2 - \frac{1}{\epsilon}}, \tag{D.5.12}$$

$$\frac{s_d}{\epsilon} = \frac{\hat{q}_f - \left(1 - \frac{1}{\epsilon}\right)q_d}{q_d + \hat{q}_f}, \tag{D.5.13}$$

$$\frac{s_f}{\epsilon} = \frac{q_d - \left(1 - \frac{1}{\epsilon}\right)\hat{q}_f}{q_d + \hat{q}_f}. \tag{D.5.14}$$

From (D.5.12) for a meaningful solution to exist one must have $\epsilon > 1/2$. Total differentiation of (D.5.12)–(D.5.14) yields

$$dD = -\frac{\epsilon x(d\hat{q}_f + dq_d)}{p\left(2 - \frac{1}{\epsilon}\right)}, \tag{D.5.15}$$

$$dx_f = -\frac{x}{p\left(2 - \frac{1}{\epsilon}\right)}\{[(1 + s_f)\epsilon - s_d]d\hat{q}_f + (s_f - \epsilon s_d)dq_d\}, \tag{D.5.16}$$

$$dx_d = -\frac{x}{p\left(2 - \frac{1}{\epsilon}\right)}\{[(1 + s_d)\epsilon - s_f]dq_d + (s_d - \epsilon \hat{s}_f)d\hat{q}_f\}. \tag{D.5.17}$$

Finally, by totally differentiating (D.5.10) and (D.5.11) and substituting (D.5.15)–(D.5.17) into the results, we obtain

$$\left[2\left(2 - \epsilon - \frac{1}{\epsilon}\right)\hat{q}_f + \left(2 + \epsilon - \frac{2}{\epsilon}\right)q_d - (1 - \epsilon)c'_f\right]d\hat{q}_f$$

$$+ \left[\left(2 + \epsilon - \frac{2}{\epsilon}\right)\hat{q}_f - 2q_d - \left(2 + \epsilon - \frac{1}{\epsilon}\right)c'_f\right]dq_d$$

$$= c'_f\left[(1 - \epsilon)\hat{q}_f + q_d\left(2 + \epsilon - \frac{1}{\epsilon}\right)\right]dt \tag{D.5.18}$$

$$\left[2\left(2 - \epsilon - \frac{1}{\epsilon}\right)q_d + \left(2 + \epsilon - \frac{2}{\epsilon}\right)\hat{q}_f - (1 - \epsilon)c'_d\right]dq_d$$

$$+ \left[\left(2 + \epsilon - \frac{2}{\epsilon}\right)q_d - 2\hat{q}_f - \left(2 + \epsilon - \frac{1}{\epsilon}\right)c'_d\right]d\hat{q}_f = 0. \tag{D.5.19}$$

Since the simplifying assumptions made so far are still not enough for us to obtain clear-cut results, we further assume that the domestic and the foreign producers have the same level of marginal costs, i.e., $c_f = c_d = c$. This assumption enables us to obtain the closed-form solutions of q_f and

q_d (when $t = 0$) as

$$q_f = q_d = q = \frac{(3\epsilon - 1)c}{3(\epsilon - 1)}. \tag{D.5.20}$$

In view of (D.5.20), equations (D.5.18) and (D.5.19) are simplified to

$$A d\hat{q}_f + B dq_d = \frac{c(3\epsilon - 1)^2}{\epsilon} dt, \tag{D.5.21}$$

$$B d\hat{q}_f + A dq_d = 0, \tag{D.5.22}$$

where

$$A = \left(6 - \epsilon - \frac{4}{\epsilon}\right)(3\epsilon - 1) + 3(1 - \epsilon)^2,$$

and

$$B = \left(\epsilon - \frac{2}{\epsilon}\right)(3\epsilon - 1) - 3\left(2 + \epsilon - \frac{1}{\epsilon}\right)(\epsilon - 1).$$

Solving dq_f from (D.5.21) and (D.5.22) and then dx_f and dx_d from (D.5.16) and (D.5.17), and substituting all these into (5.34), one obtains

$$\frac{\Omega\left(2 - \frac{1}{\epsilon}\right)}{(3\epsilon - 1)xc} \frac{dW_h}{dt}\bigg|_{t=0} = \frac{25\epsilon^4 - 2\epsilon^3 - 33\epsilon^2 + 22\epsilon - 4}{\epsilon^3}, \tag{D.5.23}$$

where Ω is equal to $B^2 - A^2$ and has to be negative for the stability of the system.

6   Foreign penetration in the presence of unemployment

6.1   Introduction

As the globalization of the world economy continued over the last decade or so, the world witnessed phenomenal increases in the volume of foreign direct investment (FDI). According to the International Monetary Fund, FDI to developing and transitional economies grew from US$18.6 billion in 1990 to US$83.0 billion in 1995 (see IMF, 1996). This trend is likely to continue. The increased importance of FDI is now well recognized and many rules on FDI have been incorporated in the Articles of the World Trade Organization (WTO) set up in 1995. One of the remits of the WTO is to eliminate impediments to FDI.

In this and the following chapters of this book we deal extensively with various aspects of FDI, such as employment promotion, international inflow and outflow of firms, and lobbying for FDI, and we investigate the properties of a number of alternative optimal policies towards FDI such as profit taxes, local content restrictions, and FDI-promoting subsidies.

The theoretical literature on FDI is very large with several strands and ramifications. Broadly speaking, there are three strands in the literature coming respectively from international trade theory (see, for example, Brander and Spencer, 1987; Dixit, 1984; Ethier, 1986; Ethier and Horn, 1990; Glass and Saggi, 1999; Helpman, 1984b; Hillman and Ursprung, 1993; Hortsmann and Markusen, 1987, 1992; Katrak, 1977; Lahiri and Ono, 1998a, 1998b, 2003; Motta, 1992; Ono, 1990; Petit and SannaRandaccio, 2000; Smith, 1987; Yabuuchi, 1997), public finance (see, for example, Devereux and Griffith, 1996; Haufler, 2001; Haufler and Schjelderup, 2000; Haufler and Wooton, 1999; Janeba, 1995; Keen, 1991; Wildasin, 1989), and international business organization (see, for example, Casson and Pearce, 1987; Dunning, 1993). There is now a dominant framework of analysis for FDI, namely the ownership–location–internationalization (OLI) paradigm or 'eclectic' theory as Dunning called it. Most of the papers cited above can be fitted into one or more of the above three (O, L or I) categories. An important question in the literature is location: when does it pay a multinational enterprise (MNE) to locate one of its plants in a particular host country to serve the market there rather than to export the commodity to that country after producing it in the home country of the MNE?

The purpose of the following analysis is not to provide yet another rationale for FDI. Rather it focuses on the welfare effect of FDI in the presence of oligopoly. First, this chapter examines the effect of FDI on the host country's welfare via two channels, employment promotion and price change. Subsequent chapters will deal with other issues.

In chapter 3 we examined the scope for government policies towards foreign penetration either by FDI or by exports. In particular, it explored the welfare effect of a restriction on the foreign firm's output. However, the analysis was conducted under the assumption of full employment. In reality, a country's attitude towards foreign penetrations is guided more often than not by its effect on domestic employment. Therefore, a proper analysis of foreign penetration requires a model that incorporates the presence of unemployment.[1] This is precisely what is done in the present chapter. That is, by extending the model of chapter 3 to a model that accommodates unemployment, this chapter analyses the effect of foreign penetration on the domestic welfare and examines the optimal restriction on foreign penetration.

In the presence of unemployment there is a discrepancy between the social and the private production costs. When a firm employs labour, it has to pay wages, which are private costs. However, the opportunity or social cost of labour is zero in the presence of unemployment since the firm can raise production by hiring more labour without reducing the employment and thus the production of any other firm. Thus, while computing the level of welfare in an economy with unemployment, one has to add wage income to producers' and consumers' surplus so that the private costs used to calculate producers' surplus get changed into social surplus.

Foreign penetration through FDI has both positive and negative effects on domestic employment. It generates new job opportunities but at the same time reduces domestic firms' employment since FDI causes domestic firms to decrease production. Thus, when considering an industrial policy on FDI, one must take into account which of the two effects is larger. Foreign penetration via exports has a negative effect on domestic employment only by reducing domestic production. Both types of foreign penetration however benefit domestic consumers by reducing the domestic price and thus increasing consumers' surplus.

---

[1] See, for example, Brander and Spencer (1987) and Lahiri and Ono (1998a, b and 2003) for models of FDI with unemployment.

Section 6.2 develops the basic model and examines the welfare effect of restricting the output of a foreign firm that has established a foreign subsidiary in a host country. In other words, foreign penetration analysed in section 6.2 is assumed to be through FDI and the sector is taken to be non-tradeable. Having established some general results in section 6.2, section 6.3 will consider the special case of linear demand and cost functions and derive more specific results. Section 6.4 will then consider the case where domestic firms face foreign penetration through trade and the domestic government restricts the level of exports by the foreign firm. Finally, in section 6.5 some concluding remarks will be made.

6.2   Foreign direct investment and national welfare

Suppose that there are n domestic firms in the market. The demand function is given by

$$D = D(p) \Longleftrightarrow p = f(D), \quad f'(D) < 0, \tag{6.1}$$

where p and D denote price and demand respectively and f denotes the inverse demand function. Profits π_i for a domestic firm i ($i = 1, \ldots, n$) is represented by

$$\pi_i = f(D)x_i - c_i(x_i), \tag{6.2}$$

where x_i and $c_i(\cdot)$ denote the output and the total cost of firm i, respectively. If the government restricts the foreign firm's production to Q, total demand D is

$$D = X + Q \quad \text{where} \quad X = \sum_{i=1}^{n} x_i. \tag{6.3}$$

Maximizing π_i, firm i determines x_i that satisfies

$$\frac{\partial \pi_i}{\partial x_i} = f(D) + f'(D)x_i(1 + \delta_i) - c_i'(x_i) = 0, \tag{6.4}$$

where δ_i, which represents firm i's conjectural variation of the rival firms' total output, is constant. As mentioned in chapter 3, it is assumed that

$$\delta_i > -1 \quad \text{for} \quad i = 1, \ldots, n. \tag{6.5}$$

It is to be noted that in the case of a Cournot oligopoly,

$$\delta_i = 0 \quad \text{for} \quad i = 1, \ldots, n.$$

As in chapter 3, we also make the 'normal' assumptions here (see assumption 3.1 of chapter 3). That is,

Assumption 6.1

$$f + f''(D)x_i(1+\delta_i) < 0, \ (1+\delta_i)f' - c_i'' < 0, \ \text{for all } i.$$

From (6.3) and (6.4), we find

$$\frac{dx_i}{dQ} = -\frac{f' + f''(D)x_i(1+\delta_i)}{\{(1+\delta_i)f' - c_i''\}\left[1 + \sum_{j=1}^{n}\frac{f'+f''(D)x_j(1+\delta_j)}{(1+\delta_j)f'-c_j''}\right]}. \tag{6.6}$$

Thus, under assumption 6.1

$$\frac{dx_i}{dQ} < 0. \tag{6.7}$$

Using (6.1), (6.3), (6.6) and assumption 6.1, we also find

$$\frac{dp}{dQ} = \frac{f'}{1 + \sum_{j=1}^{n}\frac{f'+f''(D)x_j(1+\delta_j)}{(1+\delta_j)f'-c_j''}} < 0. \tag{6.8}$$

Equations (6.7) and (6.8) confirm our earlier assertion that an increased foreign penetration in the form of a higher Q reduces domestic production X, but also reduces domestic price p.

Turning to welfare, domestic producers' surplus W_p is

$$W_p = \sum_{i=1}^{n}[px_i - c_i(x_i)],$$

from which a change in W_p is obtained as

$$dW_p = \sum_{i=1}^{n}[p - c_i(x_i)]dx_i + \sum_{i=1}^{n}x_i dp. \tag{6.9}$$

A change in consumer's surplus W_c is given by

$$dW_c = -Ddp. \tag{6.10}$$

In addition to W_p and W_c, there are also wage earnings W_L paid by domestic firms and W_L^* paid by foreign firms:

$$W_L = \sum_{i=1}^{n}c_i(x_i), \quad W_L^* = c_f(Q), \tag{6.11}$$

where $c_f(\cdot)$ is the total cost function of the foreign firm.

Since labour employed in the sector under consideration would be left unemployed unless the domestic and foreign firms utilized it, total domestic surplus W is given by[2]

$$W = W_c + W_p + W_L + W_L^*.$$

---

[2] See also Brander and Spencer (1987) for this specification of total surplus.

From (6.3), (6.4) and (6.9)–(6.11), a change in domestic total surplus W is obtained as

$$
\begin{aligned}
dW &= \sum_{i=1}^{n}[p - c_i'(x_i)]dx_i - \left(D - \sum_{i=1}^{n} x_i\right)dp \\
&\quad + \sum_{i=1}^{n} c_i'(x_i)dx_i + c_f'(Q)dQ \\
&= p\sum_{i=1}^{n} dx_i - Qdp + c_f'(Q)dQ \\
&= pdX - Qdp + c_f'(Q)dQ,
\end{aligned}
\tag{6.12}
$$

where $dX = \sum_{i=1}^{n} dx_i$.

From (6.7) and (6.12) it is clear that if both $c_f'(Q)$ and Q are small enough, dW/dQ is negative. Thus,

Proposition 6.1 *Suppose that a country in which unemployment exists faces FDI and that its government restricts the foreign (subsidiary) firm's supply so as to protect domestic firms. Under assumption 6.1, if the marginal cost of the foreign firm is sufficiently small, there is a restriction level below which more restrictions on the foreign firm's supply always increase total surplus for the host country.*

The intuition for this proposition is similar to that for proposition 3.1 in chapter 3. Because of the presence of unemployment here, there is an additional effect. A restriction on the foreign firm's supply raises the domestic firms' employment and decreases the foreign firm's employment. Thus, if the foreign firm is very efficient and hires a small amount of labour, the restriction raises the total employment and thus raises the beneficial effect in comparison to the case of full employment. However, if the foreign firm is inefficient and thus hires a large number of workers, the restriction reduces the total employment. Therefore, the beneficial effect of restricting the foreign firm's supply is lower in the presence of unemployment than in the absence of it. Note that if the foreign firm supplies its products through trade, it hires no domestic labour and therefore the beneficial effect of the restriction becomes larger than in the case of penetration through FDI. We shall examine the case of penetration through exports in section 6.4.

Having derived a general result in the above proposition, we shall in the next section consider the special case of linear demand and cost functions and a Cournot oligopoly in order to derive sharper results.

6.3   A linear case

In this section the sector under consideration is assumed to be Cournot oligopolistic so that $\delta_i = 0$ for any i. Furthermore, it is assumed that the domestic demand function is

$$p = \alpha - \beta D, \tag{6.13}$$

and that the total cost functions of domestic firm i and the foreign firm are

$$c_i = \gamma x_i, \quad c_f = \gamma_f Q, \tag{6.14}$$

where, for simplicity, the marginal (and average) cost is the same for all domestic firms.

Substituting (6.13) and (6.14) into (6.4) and rearranging the terms yield

$$\beta x_i = \alpha - \gamma - \beta D, \quad \text{for} \quad i = 1, \ldots, n. \tag{6.15}$$

From (6.3) and (6.15), the equilibrium value of demand D is obtained as a function of Q:

$$D = \frac{\beta Q + n(\alpha - \gamma)}{(1 + n)\beta} = F(Q) \text{ (say)}. \tag{6.16}$$

Total domestic surplus W in this case is

$$W = \int_0^{F(Q)} \beta [F(Q) - D] \, dD + n[\alpha - \gamma - \beta F(Q)] x_i + n \gamma x_i + \gamma_f Q.$$

Using (6.13)–(6.16), the above expression is simplified to

$$W = \frac{\beta [F(Q)]^2}{2} + \frac{n[\alpha - \gamma - \beta F(Q)][\alpha - \beta F(Q)]}{\beta} + \gamma_f Q. \tag{6.17}$$

From (6.16) and (6.17), we find

$$\frac{dW}{dQ} = \frac{(1 + 2n)\beta Q - n(\alpha + n\gamma) + (1 + n)^2 \gamma_f}{(1 + n)^2}, \tag{6.18}$$

$$\frac{d^2 W}{dQ^2} = \frac{(1 + 2n)\beta}{(1 + n)^2} > 0. \tag{6.19}$$

Thus, W is a U-shaped function of a foreign firm's supply Q, and domestic surplus W is lowest when

$$\beta Q = \frac{n(\alpha + n\gamma) - (1 + n)^2 \gamma_f}{(1 + 2n)}. \tag{6.20}$$

It is to be noted that in order for the quantitative restriction on the foreign firm's output to be binding, one needs to make sure that under no restriction on the foreign supply the foreign firm will in fact supply to the host market. If there is no restriction on foreign supply, the first order profit-maximizing condition for the foreign firm is given by

$$\beta Q = \alpha - \gamma_f - \beta D, \tag{6.21}$$

and the foreign supply and the total demand are

$$Q = Q^* = \frac{\alpha + n\gamma - (n+1)\gamma_f}{\beta(n+2)}, \tag{6.22}$$

$$D = F(Q^*) = \frac{(n+1)\alpha - n\gamma - \gamma_f}{\beta(n+2)}. \tag{6.23}$$

From (6.22), it follows that any restriction on foreign supply cannot be binding if $\alpha + n\gamma < (n+1)\gamma_f$. Furthermore, from (6.18), it is evident that W is an increasing function of Q for all positive values of Q if γ_f is larger than $n(\alpha + n\gamma)/(n+1)^2$. Thus,

Proposition 6.2 *The more a foreign (subsidiary) firm produces, the larger the domestic welfare becomes if*

$$\frac{n(\alpha + n\gamma)}{(n+1)} \leq (n+1)\gamma_f < \alpha + n\gamma.$$

It is to be noted that the presence of unemployment plays an important role in the derivation of the above result. In particular, if γ_f is sufficiently high, the employment-creating effect of the foreign firm dominates the negative effects, thus, allowing the foreign firm to supply more increases domestic welfare.

In chapter 3 it was shown that in the absence of unemployment, domestic total surplus is lowest when the foreign share is restricted to 50% (see proposition 3.2(1)). We shall now examine how the presence of unemployment affects this result.

Since D is given by (6.16), equation (6.18) reduces to

$$(1+n)\frac{dW}{dQ} = 2\beta D\left[\frac{Q}{D} - \frac{1}{2}\right] + (1+n)\gamma_f - n\gamma. \tag{6.24}$$

From (6.24) it is clear that, in the case where $(1+n)\gamma_f > n\gamma$, welfare is minimized when the foreign share is less than 50%. That is, a more severe restriction on foreign supply is less likely to increase welfare in the presence of unemployment than in the absence of it. As mentioned before, this is due to the employment-creation effect of the foreign supply.

In chapter 3 we also showed that there is a critical share for the foreign supply and that if the permissible share is below that critical level, a total prohibition against the foreign penetration results in the highest level of domestic surplus (see proposition 3.2(2)). We shall next examine how that critical share is affected by the presence of unemployment.

Using (6.16), W given by (6.17) reduces to

$$
\begin{aligned}
W &= \frac{\beta [F(Q)]^2}{2} + \frac{n[\alpha - \gamma - \beta F(Q)]^2}{\beta} + \gamma (F(Q) - Q) + \gamma_f Q \\
&= \frac{\beta [F(Q)]^2}{2} + \frac{n[\alpha - \gamma - \beta F(Q)]^2}{\beta} \\
&\quad + (n+1)[(n+1)\gamma_f - n\gamma]F(Q) + \frac{n(\alpha - \gamma)(\gamma - \gamma_f)}{\beta}.
\end{aligned}
\tag{6.25}
$$

Turning now to the derivation of the critical share, we calculate total demand $\hat{D}$ satisfying

$$
\begin{aligned}
W &= \frac{\beta \hat{D}^2}{2} + \frac{n[\alpha - \gamma - \beta \hat{D}]^2}{\beta} + (n+1)[(n+1)\gamma_f - n\gamma]\hat{D} \\
&\quad + \frac{n(\alpha - \gamma)(\gamma - \gamma_f)}{\beta} \\
&= \frac{\beta [F(0)]^2}{2} + \frac{n[\alpha - \gamma - \beta F(0)]^2}{\beta} \\
&\quad + (n+1)[(n+1)\gamma_f - n\gamma]F(0) + \frac{n(\alpha - \gamma)(\gamma - \gamma_f)}{\beta}.
\end{aligned}
\tag{6.26}
$$

Obviously, $\hat{D}$ is the level of total demand at which W equals the welfare level that is obtained under a total prohibition against foreign penetration. From (6.26) it is clear that $\hat{D}$ satisfies

$$
\begin{aligned}
G(\hat{D}) &+ (n+1)[(n+1)\gamma_f - n\gamma]\hat{D} \\
&= \bar{F} + (n+1)[(n+1)\gamma_f - n\gamma]F(0),
\end{aligned}
\tag{6.27}
$$

where

$$
G(\hat{D}) = \frac{\beta \hat{D}^2}{2} + \frac{n[\alpha - \gamma - \beta \hat{D}]^2}{\beta},
$$

$$
\bar{F} = \frac{\beta [F(0)]^2}{2} + \frac{n[\alpha - \gamma - \beta F(0)]^2}{\beta}.
$$

Comparing (6.27) with the corresponding equation for the case with full employment, i.e., equation (3.19) in chapter 3 (with $\delta_i = 0$) which in terms of the present notation is simply $G(\hat{D}) = \bar{F}$, one can show that the critical value of $\hat{D}$ is lower in the presence of unemployment than in the absence of it if and only if $(n + 1)\gamma_f > n\gamma$. This result is formally stated and proved in the following proposition.

Proposition 6.3 *When foreign penetration is via direct investment, the critical share of a foreign firm below which a total prohibition on its supply maximizes the welfare of the host country is lower in the presence of unemployment than in the absence of it if and only if $(n + 1)\gamma_f > n\gamma$.*

Proof. Suppose that $\hat{D}$ satisfies $G(\hat{D}) = \bar{F}$ and that D^* satisfies $G(D^*) + aD^* = \bar{F} + aF(0)$ where $a = (n + 1)\gamma_f - n\gamma$. Subtracting the first equation from the second yields

$$G(D^*) - G(\hat{D}) = a[F(0) - D^*]. \tag{6.28}$$

Note that $F(0) < D^*$ and that $G(\cdot)$ is an increasing function of its argument in the region where D^* and $\hat{D}$ lie. Therefore, from (6.28), it is evident that $D^* < \hat{D}$ if and only if $a > 0$.

Furthermore, from (6.16) we can write

$$(1 + n)\beta = \beta(Q/D) + n(\alpha - \gamma)(1/D).$$

Thus, if the critical value of D is lower in a situation, so will the critical value of Q/D be. Therefore, the critical share of foreign supply below which the total prohibition against foreign penetration is optimal is lower in the case when there is unemployment than when there is not if and only if $(n + 1)\gamma_f > n\gamma$. □

The intuition for this result is similar to the one given before in this chapter. The employment effect of foreign supply is large when the marginal cost of production of the foreign firm is sufficiently high and this effect dominates some of the negative effects of foreign supply via reduction in employment by the domestic firms.

We shall conclude this section by comparing the welfare level under a total prohibition, i.e., $Q = 0$, with that under no restriction, i.e., $Q = Q^*$, see (6.22). From (6.22) and (6.23), we find that, without any restriction on FDI, domestic firms will supply positive amounts if and only if [3]

$$\gamma_f > 2\gamma - \alpha. \tag{6.29}$$

---

[3] By equating Q to D in (6.22) and (6.23), we get $\gamma_f = 2\gamma - \alpha$. Therefore, domestic production cannot be positive if $\gamma_f \leq 2\gamma - \alpha$.

Substituting (6.22) into (6.17) we obtain $W(Q^*)$ and then derive

$$W(Q^*) - W(0) = \left[(n+1)\gamma_f - \frac{(\alpha + n\gamma)(2n^2 + 2n - 1)}{(2n^2 + 4n + 3)} \right]$$
$$\times \frac{(2n^2 + 4n + 3) Q^*}{2(n+1)^2(n+2)}, \tag{6.30}$$

whence using (6.29) the following proposition follows.

Proposition 6.4 *No restriction on FDI is the best policy if*

$$\frac{(\alpha + n\gamma)(2n^2 + 2n - 1)}{(2n^2 + 4n + 3)} \leq (n+1)\gamma_f \quad and \quad \gamma_f > 2\gamma - \alpha.$$

The intuition is once again similar to the ones given before in this section. When the marginal cost of the foreign firm is sufficiently high, the employment–promotion effect of FDI is so large that it dominates the reduction in the domestic firms' employment caused by the increase in the foreign firm's supply.

6.4   Penetration through trade

We have so far treated the case of foreign penetration through FDI where foreign firms use domestic unemployed labour, causing domestic welfare to increase. In contrast, in the present section we shall consider the case where foreign penetration is via exports from the foreign country to the host country. Since foreign firms do not employ domestic labour, foreign penetration benefits the domestic country only through a price effect and harms the domestic country by reducing domestic production and thus employment and profits.

In this case a change in domestic welfare W is given by

$$dW = p\,dX - Q\,dp. \tag{6.31}$$

Comparing the above equation with the corresponding equation for the case of FDI (equation (6.12)), we note that this is a special case of FDI in which the foreign subsidiary's marginal cost is zero. Therefore, proposition 6.1 is strengthened in the present case by removing the qualification there on the size of the marginal cost of the foreign firm. It is done in proposition 6.5 below.

Proposition 6.5 *In the case of foreign penetration through trade there is a restriction level below which more restrictions on the foreign firm's supply always increase total surplus for the host country.*

The intuition for the above result is similar to that of proposition 3.1 in chapter 3.

Having derived a general result, we shall now derive some of the critical shares analysed in section 6.3 in the case of foreign penetration through trade. We assume a Cournot oligopoly, i.e., $\delta_i = 0$ for all i, and linearity of demand and cost functions – equations (6.13) and (6.14).

In this case total domestic surplus W takes the value given by (6.26) in which γ_f is zero. In fact, from (6.13)–(6.15), total domestic surplus W is obtained as

$$W = \frac{\beta [F(Q)]^2}{2} + \frac{n[\alpha - \gamma - \beta F(Q)][\alpha - \beta F(Q)]}{\beta}. \qquad (6.32)$$

From (6.16) and (6.32) we find

$$\frac{dW}{dQ} = \frac{(1 + 2n)\beta Q - n(\alpha + n\gamma)}{(1 + n)^2}, \qquad (6.33)$$

$$\frac{d^2 W}{dQ^2} = \frac{(1 + 2n)\beta}{(1 + n)^2} > 0. \qquad (6.34)$$

Thus, W is a U-shaped function of foreign supply Q, and is lowest when

$$\beta Q = \frac{n(\alpha + n\gamma)}{(1 + 2n)}. \qquad (6.35)$$

In this case the critical share s_f of foreign supply (below which an increase in foreign penetration is harmful) is

$$s_f = \frac{Q}{F(Q)} = \frac{1}{2} + \frac{\gamma \left(\frac{1}{2} + n\right)}{2\alpha - \gamma} > \frac{1}{2}. \qquad (6.36)$$

Recall that in the absence of unemployment the critical share is 50%. In the case of unemployment and foreign penetration through FDI the critical share is less than 50% when $(n + 1)\gamma_f > n\gamma$. In the present case, the share is unambiguously bigger than 50%, i.e., the range of foreign supply over which it is beneficial to encourage further foreign penetration is smaller in the present case than in the case of full employment. This is because in the present case foreign penetration has an additional negative effect on domestic employment, as compared to the case of full employment.

We now turn to the derivation of the critical share of foreign supply below which a total prohibition of foreign penetration is beneficial. By substituting $\gamma_f = 0$ into (6.27), we calculate total demand $\hat{D}$ satisfying

$$G(\hat{D}) - n\gamma(n + 1)\hat{D} = \bar{F} - n\gamma(n + 1)F(0), \qquad (6.37)$$

where $G(\cdot)$ and $\bar{F}$ are defined in (6.27). Needless to say, this $\hat{D}$ is the level of total demand at which domestic welfare W takes the same level as is obtained when there is no foreign supply.

Comparing (6.37) with (3.19) in chapter 3 (with $\delta_i = 0$) and (6.27), and using the logic of the proof in proposition 6.3, the following two propositions follow.

Proposition 6.6 *When foreign penetration is via exports, the critical share of a foreign firm below which a total prohibition on its supply maximizes the host country's welfare is higher in the presence of unemployment than in the absence of it.*

Proposition 6.7 *In the presence of unemployment, the critical share below which a total prohibition on foreign penetration is beneficial, is higher when the penetration is through exports than when it is through direct investment.*

Proposition 6.6 is a special case of proposition 6.3 with $\gamma_f = 0$, and proposition 6.7 follows from a direct comparisons between (6.27) and (6.37).

Finally, we compare the welfare level under a complete restriction ($Q = 0$) with that under 100% penetration ($D = Q$). From (6.16), when the foreign firm has a 100% share, its supply is

$$Q' = \frac{(\alpha - \gamma)}{\beta}. \tag{6.38}$$

From (6.16), (6.32) and (6.38), we obtain

$$W(Q') - W(0) = \frac{(\alpha - \gamma)[\alpha - (2n^2 + 2n + 1)\gamma]}{[2\beta(1 + n)^2]}.$$

From the above equation proposition 6.8 follows.

Proposition 6.8 *If under no restriction on its supply the foreign firm captures 100% of the domestic market, a total import restriction is the best policy if and only if*

$$\alpha < (2n^2 + 2n + 1)\gamma.$$

Proposition 6.8 shows that unless domestic firms hire very little labour, i.e., their marginal costs are very low, the government should totally prohibit imports. In the case of FDI, foreign firms hire domestic labour, causing domestic welfare to increase. Therefore, accepting FDI may well benefit the domestic country, as shown in proposition 6.4. Foreign penetration through trade, in contrast, does not directly raise employment but in fact reduces employment generated by domestic firms. If the marginal costs of the domestic firms are very low, this negative effect of foreign penetration is not significant and a total prohibition against imports is not advisable. Otherwise prohibiting foreign penetration benefits the domestic country.

6.5   Conclusion

Foreign penetration in a market normally takes two forms. First, foreign firms often set up subsidiaries in a host country to serve the market there. This is foreign penetration by FDI. Alternatively, a foreign firm may decide to stay in the home country and serve the market in another country by directly exporting its output there. This is foreign penetration by exports. In this chapter we have analysed the efficacy or otherwise of a host country's attempt to restrict foreign penetration of both types described above when the host country faces unemployment. In particular, we analysed the properties of two critical shares: (1) the share of foreign supply below which a restriction on foreign penetration is welfare improving, and (2) the share of foreign supply below which a total prohibition against foreign penetration is welfare improving.

The presence of unemployment brings in a number of new issues that were absent in the analysis of chapter 3. FDI creates new job openings in the host country, which is socially beneficial as the new employees would have remained unemployed otherwise. However, FDI also has some negative impact on employment as FDI crowds out employment by domestic rival firms to some extent. The net effect of FDI on employment then depends on the nature of technologies employed by the foreign firms vis-à-vis those employed by the domestic firms. In contrast, foreign penetration through trade creates employment in the home country, reduces the share of domestic firms and thus decreases employment in the host country. Both types of penetration have a common price-reducing beneficial effect on the host country.

Because of the above mechanisms through employment creation and destruction, we find that the critical shares are different in the present case than in the case where there is no unemployment. Furthermore, the critical shares also depend on the nature of foreign penetration. In the case of foreign penetration through trade, the presence of unemployment makes the critical shares higher. A prohibition against foreign penetration is more likely beneficial to the importing country. When foreign penetration is via FDI, the shares are lower in the presence of unemployment if the marginal costs of the foreign firms are sufficiently high, because such foreign firms require a large amount of labour input and thus create significant employment.

7   Local content requirement and profit taxation

7.1   Introduction

With rapid globalization of the world economy, increasingly many countries are encouraging inward foreign direct investment (FDI). In fact, one can say that 'demand' for FDI now significantly exceeds 'supply' of it. As a result, there is a fierce competition for foreign investment, whether direct or indirect, and in recent years a significant theoretical and empirical literature has developed on 'tax competitions': host countries using tax instruments to attract foreign investment (see, for example, Devereux and Griffith, 1996; Keen, 1991; Wildasin, 1989), although in the bulk of this literature foreign investment is of the portfolio type and is not FDI.[1]

In chapter 6 we analysed the effect of restricting FDI on the host country's welfare when only one foreign firm takes part in FDI. By introducing free entry and exit of foreign firms to the model of chapter 6, this chapter considers the host country's optimal policies to attract FDI. There are many instruments that a host country government can use to encourage or discourage foreign firms, and to make the best use of the foreign firms. One of such instruments is to specify that at least a certain fraction of inputs should be bought in the local market. This restriction on the input use is called the local content requirement. A profit tax on foreign firms also affects their entry and exit.

There are several reasons for a host country to encourage FDI. For example, it may want to provide a commodity to its nationals at a price which the domestic firms cannot (or do not) provide. Incoming FDI may also create new job opportunities by increasing demand for local intermediate and primary inputs in general and labour in particular. Therefore,

---

[1] Foreign investment is, broadly speaking, of two types: (i) FDI where a firm locates its plant in a foreign country along with the necessary managerial resources, and (ii) portfolio investment where a firm simply owns a part of the capital stock of a foreign firm. In the latter type, which is prevalent in the literature of tax competitions, foreign investment is equivalent to international mobility of capital as a factor of production (see Ruffin, 1984 for a survey of the theoretical literature on international factor movements).

FDI inflows are desired especially by countries with a serious unemployment problem. Also, there are many reasons for a country to discourage FDI. For example, FDI can have damaging effects on local competing firms, as has been seen in chapter 6.

From the above discussion three points are clear in formulating appropriate policies: (1) a host country needs to balance the costs and benefits of FDI, (2) the number, and the efficiency level, of domestic firms must play an important role, and (3) a host country can make use of non-tax instruments such as specification on 'local content' of inputs in order to enhance benefits from FDI.

Local content requirements have been increasing in popularity in developed and developing countries alike (see UNIDO, 1986), because no new jobs are created in the host country if the foreign firm uses only the inputs produced in its home country. The automobile industries, for example, in many countries are subject to these regulations (see Herander and Thomas, 1986). There are numerous other examples of these regulations in other industries, the oil-refining industry in the United States of America being just another example (see Krugman and Obstfeld, 1994, pp. 212–14). The World Trade Organization is very much cognizant of the fact that local content requirements are used pervasively to restrict the international mobility of capital and has incorporated in the WTO Treaty elimination of them as one of its long term objectives. Given the prevalence of local content requirements, it is surprising that the existing literature has ignored this as a possible instrument for the host country.[2]

In this chapter we consider a partial equilibrium model of an oligopolistic industry in which a number of domestic and foreign firms compete in the market for a non-tradeable commodity in a host country. The number of domestic firms is fixed, but the number of foreign firms, and hence FDI, can be affected by the government in the host country with the use of two instruments: a profit tax on the foreign firms and a variable which specifies the local content of inputs of the foreign firms.[3] The FDI

---

[2] Since the work of Grossman (1981), a small theoretical literature on content protection has developed (see Davidson, Matusz and Kreinin, 1985; Krishna and Itoh, 1988; Lopez-de-Silanes, Markusen and Rutherford, 1996; Richardson, 1991, 1993). In none of these papers, however, is the question of the optimal level of local content considered. Moreover, final goods are taken to be competitive in Grossman (1981), Krishna and Itoh (1988) and Richardson (1991, 1993), and in the cases where the final goods are imperfectly competitive (Davidson, Matusz and Kreinin, 1985; Lopez-de-Silanes, Markusen and Rutherford, 1996), only one foreign firm is considered. More recent contributions to this literature include Lahiri and Ono (1998a, b and 2003) and Qiu and Tao (2001).

[3] In the existing literature on FDI the 'outside option' of the foreign firms is to export rather than to make FDI in a particular country; in this chapter the outside option is implicitly to take FDI to some other country.

equilibrium is specified by equating the profits of the foreign firms to an exogenous level representing the reservation level of profits which the foreign firms could obtain if they penetrated alternative markets. Under the above specification of the model structure, we derive the properties of the optimal levels of the policy instruments. Among the important contributions of the chapter are the consideration of a local content requirement as a policy variable and to allow for the number of foreign firms to be endogenous, none of which can be found in the literature.

The model is spelt out in detail in the following section. Section 7.3 derives the properties of the optimal policy mix of the profit tax and the local content requirement. Finally, some concluding remarks are made in section 7.4.

7.2   The model

We consider a partial equilibrium model of an oligopolistic industry in which there are m identical domestic firms and n identical foreign firms. The marginal costs of the domestic and foreign firms are c and c^f respectively. These marginal costs are taken to be constants, and therefore they are also the average variable costs. As an extreme assumption, we take that a foreign firm would prefer to use inputs from its home country as it is cheaper to do so, but the host country stipulates that at least a proportion δ of total inputs has to be bought from the local market.

Let k (k^f) be the average variable or marginal cost of production for a foreign firm if all the inputs are bought from the host (home) economy. With the aforesaid stipulation on local contents, the marginal cost of a foreign firm is given by

$$c^f = (1 - \delta)k^f + \delta k, \tag{7.1}$$

$$\text{where} \quad k > k^f. \tag{7.2}$$

The $m + n$ firms compete in the domestic market of a non-tradeable commodity. The inverse demand function for this commodity is given by

$$p = f(D), \quad f' < 0, \tag{7.3}$$

where p and D are respectively the price and the domestic demand, the latter being the sum of outputs by the domestic and foreign firms:

$$D = mx + nx^f, \tag{7.4}$$

where x and x^f are respectively the output of a domestic and that of a foreign firm. Profits of a domestic and a foreign firm $-\pi$ and π^f respectively $-$

are given by

$$\pi = (p - c)x, \tag{7.5}$$
$$\pi^f = (p - c^f)x^f(1 - s), \tag{7.6}$$

where s is the rate of the profit tax that the host government imposes on the foreign firms.[4]

The number of the domestic firms m is assumed to be fixed.[5] However, the number of the foreign firms located in the host country, n, is endogenous and the government in the host country can affect n by changing the values of profit tax rate s and/or local content parameter δ. We assume that the host country is small in the market for FDI, i.e., foreign firms would move into (out of) the host country if the profits they make in the host country, π^f, are larger (smaller) than the reservation profit ($\bar{\pi}$) that they can make in the rest of the world. In the FDI equilibrium therefore one must have

$$\pi^f = \bar{\pi}. \tag{7.7}$$

The firms – domestic and foreign – are assumed to behave in a Cournot-Nash fashion, and therefore the first-order profit maximization conditions are

$$f(D) + f'x = c, \tag{7.8}$$
$$f(D) + f'x^f = c^f. \tag{7.9}$$

We assume, as in Brander and Spencer (1987) and chapter 6, that there is unemployment in the host country. In this case both the domestic and foreign firms' input costs paid to the host country are taken to be the host country's income. Therefore, the welfare of the host country, W, is

$$W = m\pi + sn\pi^f + mcx + n\delta kx^f + CS \tag{7.10}$$
$$= mpx + ns(p - c^f)x^f + CS + n\delta kx^f, \tag{7.11}$$

where the third and the fourth terms in (7.10) are the income of the underemployed factors, the second term is the government tax revenue, the first term denotes the profits of the domestic firms, and CS is consumers'

---

[4] Implicitly, we assume that profit taxation is source based rather than residence based, and that the home government does not give credits to firms on taxes paid abroad. Moreover, we also rule out the possibility that the host government reneges on tax promises to the foreign firms once the 'irreversible' capital investments have been made by the latter. The possibility of reneging may give rise to an equilibrium in which the foreign firms enjoy tax holidays, i.e., tax concessions for a limited period after entry (see, for example, Doyle and van Wijnbergen, 1994).

[5] In chapter 10, we shall allow the number of both domestic and foreign to be endogenous.

surplus. It is well known that

$$dCS = -Ddp. \tag{7.12}$$

This completes the model specification and we turn to its analysis. Totally differentiating the above equations, the welfare equation is written as (the details of the derivation are given in appendix E)

$$\theta dW = Bd\delta + Cds, \tag{7.13}$$

where

$$\theta = (1 - s)f'x^f(1 + \Delta^f),$$
$$B = (1 - s)x^f[2(k - k^f)m\Delta\{-p + s(p - c^f) + \delta k\}$$
$$+ 2(k - k^f)(p - c^f)\{s + n(1 - s)\} + 2(k - k^f)\delta k$$
$$- n\{k - s(k - k^f)\}(p - c^f)(1 + \Delta^f)],$$
$$C = (p - c^f)x^f[m\Delta\{-p + s(p - c^f) + \delta k\}$$
$$+ (p - c^f)s + \delta k - n(1 - s)(p - c^f)\Delta^f],$$

where Δ and Δ^f are defined in (E.7.3).

Equation (7.13) forms the backbone for the following analysis.

7.3 Optimal policies

In this section we shall characterize the optimal combination of profit tax s and local content requirement δ, and examine the relationship between the optimal (s, δ) level and the number, and the relative efficiency levels, of the domestic firms in the industry. In particular, we shall examine when the host government should encourage (discourage) FDI by subsidizing (taxing) the profits of the foreign firms. We shall also examine what sort of restrictions, if any, should be imposed with regard to local contents of inputs. In other words, we obtain the optimal values for δ and s and examine how sensitive these optimal values are to m.[6]

---

[6] Since a restriction imposed by the host government on the foreign firms' input implies a cost to the foreign firm, δ can be interpreted as a kind of production tax on the foreign firms. With this interpretation, our exercise can also be viewed as one of finding an optimal combination of *ad valorem* and specific taxation on the foreign firms; s is the *ad valorem* tax and the specific tax can be shown to be equal to $(1 - s)\delta k - \{s + \delta(1 - s)\}k^f$. In the literature on the optimal combination of *ad valorem* and specific taxation (see Delipalla and Keen, 1992; Denicolò and Matteuzzi, 2000; Myles, 1996), it is shown that an *ad valorem* tax is preferable to a specific tax. Our framework is rather different from the one analysed by Delipalla and Keen (1992) and Myles (1996) in a number of ways. First, firms are not homogeneous in our framework. Second, we suppose the presence of unemployment. Finally, as should be clear from the expression of the specific tax given above, the two tax instruments are not independent in our model. Because of these differences, our results are very different from the ones found in the existing literature.

From (7.13), we obtain

$$\frac{\partial W}{\partial \delta} = \frac{\partial W}{\partial s} = 0 \implies s^* = \frac{k - 2k^f}{k - k^f}. \tag{7.14}$$

Since $k > k^f$ from (7.2), assuming, for the time being, that the optimal solution for δ is an interior one, i.e., $0 < \delta^* < 1$, the level of optimal tax to the foreign firms is positive if and only if $k > 2k^f$. There are two main effects of the FDI policies on the host country's welfare. One is the employment effect and the other is the price-lowering effect. The first effect is large when the FDI is inefficient in the host country (i.e., k is large), and the second effect is big when the FDI is efficient (i.e., k^f and/or k is small). Therefore a large value for k has two opposing effects: higher employment and a higher price. A lower value for k^f, however, has only one effect: a lower price. If k^f is so low that $k > 2k^f$, the price-lowering effect dominates the employment effect. In this case, attracting FDI does not have a significant effect on local employment and therefore it is discouraged given that the local content parameter, which deals directly with the price-lowering effect, has an interior solution. This result is formally stated as

Proposition 7.1 *As long as $0 < \delta^* < 1$, the optimal policy for the host government is to tax the profits of the foreign firms if and only if $k > 2k^f$.*

We now turn to the determination of the optimal value of the local content parameter, δ^*, and examine when this optimal value is an interior one. From (7.13) and (7.14) we obtain

$$\frac{\theta}{2k^f x^f} \cdot \frac{\partial W}{\partial \delta}\bigg|_{s=s^*} = -\frac{(p - c^f)\Delta^f nk^f}{k - k^f} + \delta k(1 + m\Delta) - pm\Delta$$
$$+ \frac{(k - 2k^f)(p - c^f)(1 + m\Delta)}{k - k^f}. \tag{7.15}$$

In order to keep the analysis at a tractable level, we shall henceforth assume a specific form for the demand function in (7.3), viz., a linear one:

$$p = \alpha - \beta D. \tag{7.16}$$

Under this linearity assumption, welfare equation (7.15) is simplified to be (E.7.13) in appendix E. By setting the right-hand side of (E.7.13) equal to zero we obtain the optimal value, δ^*,

$$\delta^* = \frac{\frac{\{\alpha + mc - (m+1)k^f\}k^f}{k - k^f} - \left[\frac{\beta\bar{\pi}(k - k^f)}{k^f}\right]^{\frac{1}{2}} + mk^f}{k + k^f(2m + 1)}. \tag{7.17}$$

From the above expression for δ^*, the conditions under which δ^* is an interior solution are[7]

$$\delta^* < 1 \iff m(c-k) < m_1(c-k), \tag{7.18}$$

$$\delta^* > 0 \iff m(c+k-2k^f) > m_2(c+k-2k^f), \tag{7.19}$$

where the critical values of m are given as

$$m_1 = \frac{\lambda + \frac{k^2}{k^f} - \alpha}{c-k}, \tag{7.20}$$

$$m_2 = \frac{\lambda - (\alpha - k^f)}{c+k-2k^f}, \tag{7.21}$$

$$\lambda = \left[\beta\bar{\pi}\left(\frac{k-k^f}{k^f}\right)^3\right]^{\frac{1}{2}}.$$

We define $\bar{k}^f$ such that[8]

$$\psi(\bar{k}^f) = \left[\beta\bar{\pi}\left(\frac{k-\bar{k}^f}{\bar{k}^f}\right)^3\right]^{\frac{1}{2}} + \frac{k^2}{\bar{k}^f} - \alpha = 0.$$

From (7.20) we find

$$m_1(c-k) > 0 \iff k^f < \bar{k}^f. \tag{7.22}$$

Using $\bar{k}^f$ it is found that when $c = k$,

$$m > m_2 \implies \delta^* > 0; \quad m \le m_2 \implies \delta^* = 0;$$

$$k^f \ge \bar{k}^f \implies \delta^* = 1; \quad k^f < \bar{k}^f \implies \delta^* < 1. \tag{7.23}$$

Having established (7.18), (7.19) and (7.23), we are now in a position to characterize δ^* under seven possible scenarios.

Case 1 $c \ge k, \ k^f < \bar{k}^f$

In this case it can be easily shown that $m_1 > m_2$ and the relationship between the number of domestic firms, m, and δ^* is as follows (see also figure 7.1). It should be noted that when $c = k$, m_1 is infinity and hence δ^* is always less than unity.

$$m \ge m_1 \implies \delta^* = 1,$$

$$m_2 < m < m_1 \implies 0 < \delta^* < 1,$$

$$m \le m_2 \implies \delta^* = 0.$$

---

[7] It can be easily verified that the welfare function is concave.
[8] It can be shown that $\psi'(k^f) < 0$ for all $k^f \in [0, k]$, $\psi(k) < 0$ and $\psi(0) > 0$. Therefore there exists a unique $\bar{k}^f$ such that $\psi(\bar{k}^f) = 0$ and $0 < \bar{k}^f < k$.

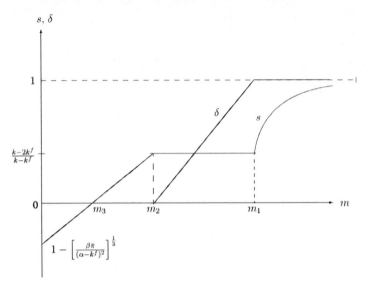

Figure 7.1   Case: $k > 2k^f$

Case 2 $c \geq k,\ \ k^f \geq \bar{k}^f$

In this case (7.22) implies that m_1 is negative. Thus, from (7.18) and (7.23), we get

$$\delta^* = 1.$$

Case 3a $c < k,\ \ k^f \leq \bar{k}^f,\ \ c + k - 2k^f > 0$

In this case m_1 is once again negative, but in view of (7.18), δ^* can never be unity. Then, from (7.19), we find

$$m > m_2 \implies 0 < \delta^* < 1,$$
$$m \leq m_2 \implies \delta^* = 0.$$

Case 3b $c < k,\ \ k^f \leq \bar{k}^f,\ \ c + k - 2k^f = 0$

Like in the previous case δ^* can never be unity here. Thus, from (7.19) and (7.21), we have

$$\alpha - \lambda - k^f > 0 \implies 0 < \delta^* < 1,$$
$$\alpha - \lambda - k^f \leq 0 \implies \delta^* = 0.$$

Case 3c $c < k,\ \ k^f \leq \bar{k}^f,\ \ c + k - 2k^f < 0$

m_1 is again negative, and therefore from (7.19), we get

$$m < m_2 \implies 0 < \delta^* < 1,$$
$$m \geq m_2 \implies \delta^* = 0.$$

Case 4a $c < k, \quad k^f > \bar{k}^f, \quad c + k - 2k^f \geq 0$

In this case it is easily shown that $m_2 < 0$, and hence the relationship between m and δ^* is

$$m > m_1 \implies 0 < \delta^* < 1,$$
$$m \leq m_1 \implies \delta^* = 1.$$

Case 4b $c < k, \quad k^f > \bar{k}^f, \quad c + k - 2k^f < 0$

In this case it is shown that $m_2 > m_1$, and then from (7.18) and (7.19), we have

$$m \leq m_1 \implies \delta^* = 1,$$
$$m_1 < m < m_2 \implies 0 < \delta^* < 1,$$
$$m \geq m_2 \implies \delta^* = 0.$$

As mentioned earlier, there are two main effects on the host country's welfare. One is the employment effect and the other is the price-lowering effect. The first effect is large when FDI is inefficient in the host country, and the second effect is large when the FDI is efficient. In case 1 the foreign firms are significantly more efficient than the domestic ones. The former can produce at a very low cost using home inputs. Therefore, by allowing the foreign firms to use inputs from home, the government can help lower the price significantly, increasing consumers' surplus. In particular, when the number of domestic firms is small $(m < m_2)$, the price-lowering effect of the foreign firms' higher efficiency outweighs its employment-reducing effect, and the government does not put any restriction on local contents $(\delta^* = 0)$. If the domestic market is more competitive $(m > m_1)$, the price-lowering effect is relatively small and the optimal local content requirement takes the highest possible value $(\delta^* = 1)$. In case 2, the foreign firms are not so efficient as in case 1. Therefore, the price-lowering effect is smaller and thus δ is set equal to unity to maximize the employment-creation effect.

Compared to cases 1 and 2, in cases 3 and 4 the foreign firms are less efficient when they use inputs solely from their home country. In case 3, as compared to case 4, k^f is lower. Therefore, the price-lowering effect is large if the foreign firms use inputs from their home country. Thus, the host country government does not forbid the foreign firms from using inputs from their home country so as to allow the price-lowering effect to have a significant impact, i.e., δ^* cannot be unity. This is particularly true in case 3a, i.e., when k^f is very small and the price-lowering effect is very large. In this case if the home market is very oligopolistic and hence m is low, the host country encourages the foreign firms to use inputs from their own countries and consequently δ^* is low. In case 3c, k^f is high relative to k, and therefore the employment effect becomes relatively important. When the number of domestic firms is low, the employment effect becomes larger, causing the optimal local content requirement δ^* to be high.

In case 4, k^f is very high. Note that k is assumed to be higher than k^f. Therefore the price-lowering effect is very small and the employment effect is important. In this case, when m is small, the employment effect is even larger, causing δ^* to be large (in fact, $\delta^* = 1$). This is true in both cases 4a and 4b. In case 4b the foreign firms are particularly inefficient. Moreover, when m is large, the market is competitive and the employment effect is small. Therefore, the government imposes no restriction on the local content ($\delta^* = 0$).

Noting that the optimal value of s is given by (7.14) only when δ^* is in the interior, it only remains for us to characterize optimal profit tax s^* when δ^* takes a corner value '0' or '1'. From (7.13), we find

$$\frac{\theta}{(p - c^f)x^f} \cdot \frac{\partial W}{\partial s} = (1 - \delta)k^f\{1 - s(1 + m)\} + \delta k\{1 + (1 + m)(1 - s)\}$$

$$- (\alpha + mc)(1 - s) + \left[\frac{\beta\bar{\pi}}{1 - s}\right]^{\frac{1}{2}}$$

$$= (1 - s)\{m(c^f - c) + (c^f - \alpha)\} + \left[\frac{\beta\bar{\pi}}{(1 - s)}\right]^{\frac{1}{2}}$$

$$- m(1 - \delta)k^f + \delta k. \tag{7.24}$$

In order to characterize s^* when $\delta^* = 0$, from (7.24) we write

$$\frac{\theta}{(p - c^f)x^f} \cdot \frac{\partial W}{\partial s}\bigg|_{\delta=0, \, s=0} = [\beta\bar{\pi}]^{\frac{1}{2}} - (\alpha - k^f + mc). \tag{7.25}$$

Assuming concavity of the welfare function, from (7.25) we find

$$s^*\big|_{\delta=0} \lesseqgtr 0 \iff m \lesseqgtr m_3, \tag{7.26}$$

where

$$m_3 = \frac{(\beta\bar{\pi})^{\frac{1}{2}} - (\alpha - k^f)}{c}.$$

That is, when $\delta^* = 0$, FDI should be discouraged if and only if the number of domestic firms is larger than a certain value. Intuitively, with $\delta^* = 0$, FDI does not bring in any benefit on account of employment. On the other hand, if the number of domestic firms is small ($m < m_3$), the price-lowering effect is important and the host country encourages FDI by subsidizing the foreign firms' profits.

Turning to the case where $\delta^* = 1$, we first obtain

$$\frac{\theta}{(p - c^f)x^f} \cdot \frac{\partial W}{\partial s}\bigg|_{\delta=1,\ s=0} = [\beta\bar{\pi}]^{\frac{1}{2}} - \{\alpha - 2k + m(c - k)\},$$

$$(7.27)$$

and then

$$s^*|_{\delta=1} \lessgtr 0 \iff m(c - k) \lessgtr m_4(c - k), \qquad (7.28)$$

where

$$m_4 = \frac{(\beta\bar{\pi})^{\frac{1}{2}} - \alpha + 2k}{c - k}.$$

That is, as in the previous case, FDI should be encouraged for sufficiently small values of m, but, this time, only if the domestic firms are less efficient than the foreign ones. Intuitively, with $\delta^* = 1$, FDI has an employment-creation effect and the domestic firms are less efficient than the foreign ones if and only if $c > k$. The above result says that when domestic competition is somewhat limited ($m < m_4$), i.e., when the price-lowering effect is strong, the optimal policy is to subsidize the relatively more efficient firms. This result is consistent with the results derived earlier in this book that the government should pick the winners (see also Lahiri and Ono, 1988, 1997).

Noting that in case 1 ($c > k$, $k < \bar{k}^f$), $m_4 > m_1$ if and only if $k < 2k^f$, the results for this case are also depicted in figures 7.1 ($k > 2k^f$) and 7.2 ($k < 2k^f$).

7.4   Conclusion

The importance of foreign direct investment (FDI) is increasingly being recognized by most countries in the world. Most of the theoretical literature on FDI focuses on the decision making of foreign firms, and the shortage of theoretical research from the perspective of the host countries is unfortunate. Moreover, in the literature that does analyse policy options facing the host countries, the choice of instruments is limited. In particular, the specification of minimum local contents in the inputs used by the foreign firms, though widespread in the real world, has not been considered. Furthermore, the number of foreign firms undertaking production in the host country is normally taken as given. This chapter contributes to the growing literature on FDI by not only considering local contents as a policy variable, but also by allowing for

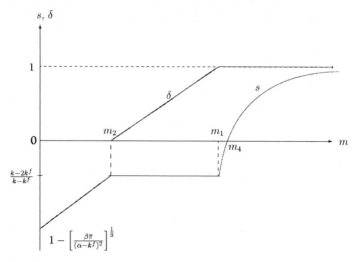

Figure 7.2   Case: $k < 2k^f$

the number of foreign firms locating themselves in the host country as endogenous.

Government policies on FDI have, broadly speaking, two effects on the host country's welfare. One is the employment effect and the other is the price-lowering effect. The first effect is large when FDI is inefficient and there are only a few firms operating in the host country. The second effect is big when the FDI is efficient, and, once again, the product market is very oligopolistic. As a result, the number of domestic firms in the host country and their relative efficiency level have important implications for the optimal structure of policies for the host country.

For example, if the foreign firms are significantly more efficient than the domestic ones when using home inputs, the government, by allowing them to use inputs from home, can help lower the price, increasing consumers' surplus. Especially in the case where the product market is highly oligopolistic, the price-lowering effect of the higher efficiency of the foreign firms outweighs its employment-reducing effect, and the government does not put any restriction on local contents. If the domestic market is more competitive, the price-lowering effect is relatively small and the optimal local content requirement takes the highest possible value. At the other extreme when the foreign firms are very inefficient relative to the domestic firms, the price-lowering effect is very small and the employment effect is important. In this case, when the number of domestic firms is small, the employment effect is even larger, causing the local content parameter to be large.

When the government decides not to put any restriction on the content of inputs for the foreign firms,[9] FDI does not bring in any benefit on account of employment. Moreover, if the number of domestic firms is small, the price-lowering effect is important and the host country encourages FDI by subsidizing the profits of the foreign firms. When the government requires the foreign firms to use inputs exclusively from the host country, FDI raises employment. If in this case the foreign firms are much more efficient than the domestic ones and hence the price-lowering effect is strong, the optimal policy is again to subsidize them.

We conclude by noting certain limitations of our analysis. First of all, we do not allow international trade in commodities,[10] and thus foreign firms do not have the option of exporting the commodity rather than establishing a firm in the host country. Second, we mostly consider the case of linear demand. Third, we only consider a quantity competition and do not allow for predatory behaviour by foreign firms.[11] Fourth, we take the number of domestic firms to be exogenous.[12] For all these reasons one must hesitate in drawing policy conclusions directly from the present analysis. Nevertheless, the results are suggestive. It is apparent that inclusion of unemployment and more importantly the instrument of local content requirement has significant implications for the nature of optimal policy towards FDI.

Appendix E

Total differentiation of (7.1), (7.8) and (7.9) leads to[13]

$$dx = -\Delta dD, \tag{E.7.1}$$

$$dx^f = -\Delta^f dD + \frac{k - k^f}{f'} d\delta, \tag{E.7.2}$$

where

$$\Delta = 1 + \frac{f''x}{f'}, \quad \Delta^f = 1 + \frac{f''x^f}{f'}. \tag{E.7.3}$$

---

[9] This chapter considers the case where the marginal cost of the foreign firms is lower when they use inputs from home than when they use inputs from the host country. Otherwise, stipulation on local content is never necessary.

[10] In chapter 8 we shall relax this assumption.

[11] However, we can appeal to the famous Kreps and Scheinkman (1983) result that the Cournot outcome holds for capacity-constrained price games.

[12] In chapter 10 we shall relax this assumption.

[13] In the literature Δ and Δ^f are normally assumed to be positive. This assumption corresponds to the 'normal' case in Seade (1980) and to strategic substitutes in Bulow, Geanakoplos and Klemperer (1985). The stability of the Cournot equilibrium is guaranteed when $1 + m\Delta + n\Delta^f$ is positive.

Differentiating (7.11) and using (7.12), (E.7.1) and (E.7.2), we find

$$dW = \left[-mp\Delta - n\{s(p - c^f) + \delta k\}\Delta^f - nx^f(1 - s)f'\right]dD$$
$$+ \left[n(k - k^f)\frac{s(p - c^f) + \delta k}{f'} + nx^f\{k - s(k - k^f)\}\right]d\delta$$
$$+ \{s(p - c^f) + \delta k\}x^f dn + n(p - c^f)x^f ds. \qquad \text{(E.7.4)}$$

Multiplying (E.7.1) by m and (E.7.2) by n, adding the two resulting equations, and using (7.4) we get

$$(1 + m\Delta + n\Delta^f)dD - \frac{n(k - k^f)}{f'}d\delta = x^f dn. \qquad \text{(E.7.5)}$$

Differentiating the FDI equilibrium condition (7.7), we find

$$(1 - s)f'x^f(1 + \Delta^f)\,dD = (p - c^f)x^f ds + 2(1 - s)x^f(k - k^f)d\delta. \qquad \text{(E.7.6)}$$

Substituting dn from (E.7.5) into (E.7.4) gives

$$dW = AdD + nx^f\{k - s(k - k^f)\}d\delta + n(p - c^f)x^f ds, \qquad \text{(E.7.7)}$$

where

$$A = m\Delta\{\delta k - (1 - s)p - sc^f\} + (p - c^f)\{s + n(1 - s)\} + \delta k.$$

Finally, substituting dD from (E.7.6) into (E.7.7), we obtain dW in terms of $d\delta$ and ds, and this is given in (7.13).

With the assumption of linear demand given by (7.16), the closed-form solutions for the following variables are

$$\bar{\pi} = (1 - s)\beta(x^f)^2, \qquad \text{(E.7.8)}$$

$$p = \frac{\alpha + nc^f + mc}{1 + n + m} = c^f + \left[\frac{\beta\bar{\pi}}{1 - s}\right]^{\frac{1}{2}}, \qquad \text{(E.7.9)}$$

$$x^f = \frac{\alpha - c^f + m(c - c^f)}{\beta(1 + n + m)} = \left[\frac{\bar{\pi}}{\beta(1 - s)}\right]^{\frac{1}{2}}, \qquad \text{(E.7.10)}$$

$$n = \left[\frac{1 - s}{\beta\bar{\pi}}\right]^{\frac{1}{2}}\{\alpha - c^f + m(c - c^f)\} - (m + 1), \qquad \text{(E.7.11)}$$

$$p - c^f = \frac{\alpha + mc - (1 + m)c^f}{1 + n + m} = \left[\frac{\beta\bar{\pi}}{1 - s}\right]^{\frac{1}{2}}. \qquad \text{(E.7.12)}$$

Substitution of (E.7.8)–(E.7.12) into (7.15) gives

$$\frac{\theta}{2k^f x^f} \cdot \frac{\partial W}{\partial \delta}\bigg|_{s=s^*} = -\frac{[\alpha - c^f + m(c - c^f)]k^f}{k - k^f} + \delta k$$

$$+ \left[\frac{\beta \bar{\pi}(k - k^f)}{k^f}\right]^{\frac{1}{2}} - m(1 - \delta)k^f, \quad \text{(E.7.13)}$$

where $c^f = (1 - \delta)k^f + \delta k$ as given by (7.1).

8   Export-oriented foreign direct investment

8.1   Introduction

Foreign firms locate themselves in a host country for a number of reasons. It could be for lower labour costs in the host country. For example, many Japanese firms make foreign direct investments in China as labour costs there are much lower than those in Japan. Typically, in such cases the commodities produced in the host country are exported in their entirety to a third country (called the consuming country).

FDI also takes place in order to have access to a market which is otherwise not penetrable. The lack of market access can be due to two reasons. The first is trade restrictions in the form of tariffs or quotas. For example, many US firms invest in Ireland and export their produce to the rest of the European Union member countries, and thus avoid the common external tariff imposed by the European Union (see, for example, Barry and Bradly, 1997). Japanese investments in the UK are also for similar reasons. The second reason is frictions between the consuming country and the home country of the foreign firms caused by massive exports directly from the home country to the consuming country. In such cases the consuming country typically imposes restrictive import quotas, and the only way the firms in the home country can export more to the consuming country is via FDI.[1]

In the above circumstances FDI often creates conflicts between the host country and the consuming country. This is because foreign penetration through FDI diminishes the market share of domestic firms in the consuming country, and this in turn has adverse effects on the level of employment and profits in that country. The host country does not lose out if there are no domestic firms, and in fact it encourages FDI inflows

---

[1] Import restrictions in the face of massive influx of imports are admissible under the World Trade Organization (WTO) rules. Consuming countries often realize that import quotas are being flouted via FDI, and regard imports from foreign subsidiaries as being part of their parent country's export when imposing import quotas. For example, the USA treats semi-conductors produced by Fujitsu in Taiwan as Japanese products.

in order to increase employment. However, foreign firms often import inputs from their home countries and therefore the host country does not benefit fully from having FDI inflows. In order to reap the full benefit of having FDI, host countries tend to impose local content requirements on foreign firms, as was seen in chapter 7. The consuming country also has an incentive for local content restrictions to be imposed on the foreign firms as they effectively reduce the competitive advantage of the latter. This is particularly so when the consuming country does not have access to instruments such as tariffs to deter market penetration by the foreign firms, as it is the case within an economic union such as the European Union.

There are many examples of conflicts of the type mentioned above. For example, the automobiles produced by Nissan in Britain have to have a certain minimum local content in order for those to be accepted as 'European' by other European Union member countries. In the late 1980s France refused to accept Nissan Bluebird as a European product, to the fury of the British government. The dispute was resolved only after Nissan agreed to raise the local content of its cars.

Before the readers form the belief that FDI is always harmful to the consuming country, we should point out that any restriction on the use of inputs by the foreign firms is clearly detrimental to the efficiency of the foreign firms and this in turn would be reflected in a higher price of the good and therefore a lower level of consumers' surplus in the consuming country. It is therefore not obvious whether the consuming country should always urge the host country to impose more severe local content restrictions on the foreign firms. Similarly, the host country can drive away foreign firms by imposing a more severe local content requirement, and thus harm itself. Therefore, both countries have to weigh the pros and cons of a local content restriction before taking any action.

In this chapter we consider a partial equilibrium model in which identical foreign firms locate themselves in a host country and export their produce in their entirety to another country, the consuming country. These firms compete with a domestic firm in the consuming country in an oligopolistic market there. We assume the existence of unemployment in both countries. We consider two cases. In the first, the number of foreign firms, and hence FDI, can be affected by the government in the host country, or by that in the consuming country via its influence on the host country's government. In particular, as mentioned above, both governments may want to stipulate that the foreign firms purchase a certain fraction of their inputs from the local markets, although the two countries would typically differ on the specific level of the restriction. In the second case, the number of foreign firms is fixed. In this case, a local content restriction would not affect the number of firms, but it would influence the output decisions of the firms.

When the number of foreign firms is endogenous, any local content restriction is bound to have a bearing on the number of firms that would enter the market. The FDI equilibrium in this case, as in chapter 7, is specified by equating the profits of the foreign firms to an exogenous level representing the reservation level of profits that the foreign firms could obtain if they penetrated alternative markets. Under the above specification of the model structure, we examine whether the consuming country should press for a more severe local content restriction than the host country.

The basic economic model structure is spelt out in detail in the following section. Section 8.3 then carries out a formal analysis. Finally, some concluding remarks are made in section 8.4.

8.2   The model

We consider a partial equilibrium model of foreign direct investment (FDI) in which there are two countries, labelled country 1 and country 2, and the rest of the world in the background. The industry under consideration is oligopolistic. n identical foreign firms from the rest of the world locate themselves in country 1 and compete with one domestic firm in country 2 for a market in the latter country.[2]

As in the analysis of the previous chapter, the marginal costs of the foreign and domestic firms, denoted respectively by c_1 and c_2, are assumed to be constant. Each foreign firm prefers to use inputs from its home country as they are cheaper, but the host country imposes a local content requirement of at least a δ proportion of total inputs. If k_1 (k_w) is the unit input cost in country 1 under the condition that all inputs are bought in the host (home) country, the marginal cost for the foreign firms under local content requirement δ is

$$c_1 = (1 - \delta)k_w + \delta k_1, \tag{8.1}$$

where $k_1 > k_w.$ (8.2)

The inverse demand function is again assumed to be

$$p = \alpha - \beta D, \quad \alpha > 0, \ \beta > 0, \tag{8.3}$$

---

[2] The assumption that there is only one domestic firm is made for simplicity and without any loss of generality. In chapter 10 we shall allow the number of both the domestic and foreign firms to be endogenous.

where p and D are respectively the price and the domestic demand. D equals the sum of outputs by the foreign firms and the domestic firm in country 2:

$$D = nx_1 + x_2, \tag{8.4}$$

where x_i $(i = 1, 2)$ is the output of a firm in country i. The profits of a firm located in country i, π_i $(i = 1, 2)$, are

$$\pi_i = (p - c_i)x_i. \tag{8.5}$$

We consider two cases depending on whether the number of the foreign firms n is exogenous or endogenous. When n is endogenous, it is affected by local content parameter δ. The foreign firms would move into and out of the host country so that in equilibrium their profits equal the outside option of profits $\bar{\pi}$, i.e.,

$$\pi_1 = \bar{\pi}. \tag{8.6}$$

Since the host country is assumed to be small in the market for FDI, $\bar{\pi}$ is taken to be constant. Since the industry is assumed to be Cournot oligopolistic, the first-order profit maximization condition is

$$p - \beta x_i = c_i, \quad i = 1, 2. \tag{8.7}$$

Furthermore, there is unemployment in countries 1 and 2 and hence the variable costs that are paid to the host country are regarded as the income of the workers who would remain unemployed if there were no foreign firms. For the same reason the entire cost of production in country 2 is assumed to be the income of workers in country 2. With this and assuming that the entire profits of the foreign firms are repatriated, the welfare levels in country 1 and 2, denoted by W_1 and W_2 respectively, are given by

$$W_1 = nx_1 \delta k_1, \tag{8.8}$$
$$W_2 = \pi_2 + c_2 x_2 + CS_2 = px_2 + CS_2, \tag{8.9}$$

where CS_2 is consumers' surplus in country 2. It is well known that

$$dCS_2 = -Ddp. \tag{8.10}$$

That is, the welfare of country 1 is given by total domestic factor income, and that of country 2 is by the sum of domestic factor income, the domestic firm's profits and consumers' surplus.

This completes the description of the model structure.

8.3   The determination of local content restriction

This section analyses the conflict of interest between countries 1 and 2 in the determination of local content parameter δ. Although it is the host country that decides δ unilaterally, in reality it is often forced to adjust δ under pressure from the consuming country. As mentioned in the introduction to this chapter, for Nissan Bluebird cars produced in the UK, France, a consuming country, forced the UK to raise the level of local content restriction. There are many such examples where a consuming country refuses to accept an imported good as being the product of the exporting country when such a good has been produced with the help of FDI. Thus, we shall examine conditions under which the consuming country would put pressure on the host country to have a more (or less) severe restriction on local content.

First, we deal with the case where the number of the foreign firms is endogenous. From the equations derived in the previous section, the variables are solved sequentially as

$$x_1 = \sqrt{\frac{\bar{\pi}}{\beta}}, \tag{8.11}$$

$$n = \frac{\alpha - 2c_1 + c_2}{\sqrt{\beta\bar{\pi}}} - 2, \tag{8.12}$$

$$x_2 = \frac{\alpha + nc_1 - (n+1)c_2}{\beta(n+2)} = \frac{\alpha + nc_1 - (n+1)c_2}{\alpha - 2c_1 + c_2} \cdot \sqrt{\frac{\bar{\pi}}{\beta}}. \tag{8.13}$$

Totally differentiating (8.1), (8.7), and (8.11)–(8.13) we get

$$\frac{dx_1}{d\delta} = 0, \tag{8.14}$$

$$\frac{1}{n+2} \cdot \frac{dn}{d\delta} = \frac{-2(k_1 - k_w)}{\alpha - 2c_1 + c_2}, \tag{8.15}$$

$$\frac{1}{x_2} \cdot \frac{dx_2}{d\delta} = \frac{(k_1 - k_w)(n+2)}{\alpha + nc_1 - (n+1)c_2}, \tag{8.16}$$

$$\frac{dp}{d\delta} = \beta \frac{dx_2}{d\delta}. \tag{8.17}$$

Since $x_2 > 0$, from (8.2), (8.12), (8.13), and (8.15)–(8.17), we find

$$\frac{dx_2}{d\delta} > 0, \quad \frac{dn}{d\delta} < 0, \quad \text{and} \quad \frac{dp}{d\delta} > 0. \tag{8.18}$$

The intuition is straightforward. Putting a more severe restriction on the foreign firms raises their marginal costs, and this reduces their number, which in turn increases the output of their rival, the domestic firm in the consuming country, and the price of the commodity.

We now turn to a welfare analysis. Differentiating (8.8) and (8.9) and making use of (8.1), (8.4), (8.10)–(8.12), (8.14), (8.15) and (8.17), we get

$$\frac{1}{W_1} \cdot \frac{dW_1}{d\delta} = \frac{-2(k_1 - k_w)}{n\sqrt{\beta\bar{\pi}}} + \frac{1}{\delta}, \tag{8.19}$$

$$\frac{dW_2}{d\delta} = (p - \beta n x_1)\frac{dx_2}{d\delta}. \tag{8.20}$$

Because of (8.14)–(8.16) and (8.18)–(8.20), $d^2W_1/d\delta^2 < 0$ and $d^2W_2/d\delta^2 > 0$. That is, W_1 is a concave function, and W_2 a convex function, of δ.[3] From (8.19) and (8.20), we find

$$\frac{3}{W_1} \cdot \frac{dW_1}{d\delta}\bigg|_{dW_2/d\delta=0} = \frac{2k_w + 2\sqrt{\beta\bar{\pi}} - \frac{\alpha+c_2}{3}}{\delta(\alpha + c_2)}. \tag{8.21}$$

There are two possibilities: either the right-hand side of (8.21) is negative, or it is positive. These two cases are depicted in figures 8.1 and 8.2 respectively. In both figures points $\hat{\delta}_1$ and $\hat{\delta}_2$ represent respectively the welfare maximizing point in country 1 and the welfare minimizing point in country 2.[4] Figure 8.1 illustrates the welfare functions in the case where the right hand side of (8.21) is negative. In the figure, point A on the welfare function of country 1 corresponds to the welfare minimizing point for country 2. At that point the welfare of country 1 is a decreasing function of δ. Point B on the welfare function of country 2 corresponds to the welfare maximizing point of country 1, and at that point the welfare function of country 2 is a decreasing function of δ. Clearly, in this case country 1 desires to set δ at $\hat{\delta}_1$, and country 2 would put pressure on country 1 to reduce the level of δ from $\hat{\delta}_1$.

By similar arguments, in figure 8.2 (which corresponds to a positive value for the right-hand side of (8.21)), country 1 desires δ to be $\hat{\delta}_1$, and country 2 would ask for an increase in the level of δ.

In view of the above discussion and (8.21), we obtain the following results.

---

[3] This property is consistent with the result in chapters 3 and 6 that under oligopoly the welfare of an importing country is a concave function of the foreign supply (see also Ono, 1990).

[4] From (8.19) it is clear that $dW_1/d\delta|_{\delta=0} > 0$ and therefore $\hat{\delta}_1 > 0$. However, in order to guarantee that $\hat{\delta}_1 < 1$, we need to assume that $4k_1 > \alpha + c_2 + 2k_w - 2\sqrt{\beta\bar{\pi}}$. In other words, k_1 should be sufficiently high for the optimal value of δ to have an interior solution.

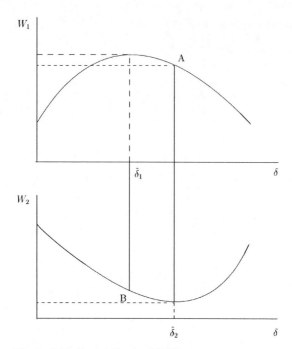

Figure 8.1 Case 1 Optimal LCRs

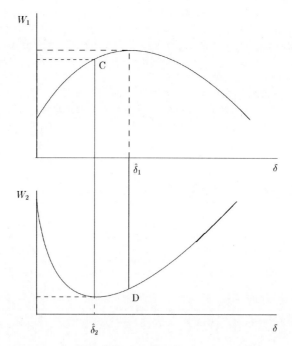

Figure 8.2 Case 2 Optimal LCRs

Proposition 8.1 *When the number of foreign firms is endogenous,*

$$\hat{\delta}_2 \lessgtr \hat{\delta}_1 \quad \Longleftrightarrow \quad 6(k_w + \sqrt{\beta\bar{\pi}}) \gtrless \alpha + c_2.$$

The above results can be explained intuitively as follows. The welfare of the host country depends entirely on the effect on employment. A more severe restriction of local content would increase employment for a given number of foreign firms. But such a policy will also drive foreign firms away, and thus reduce employment. The host country therefore has to balance these two opposing effects in choosing an appropriate level for the local content requirement. For the consuming country, a more severe restriction would give the domestic firm a competitive edge, raising its profits and output, and thus employment. However, the oligopolistic distortion and therefore the price of the good would increase, reducing consumers' surplus. When, for example, $\bar{\pi}$ is large, there would be very few foreign firms, and therefore the profit level of the domestic firm would be high. In this case, the interest of the domestic producer and the workers would dominate that of the consumers in the consuming country when calculating the total welfare of the country. Thus, it would ask for a more severe restriction on the foreign firms' local contents. On the other hand, when either α or c_2 is very high, implying a higher demand and a higher price, the consumers' interest would dominate, and the government in the consuming country would ask for a less severe requirement for local contents.

Having analysed the case of free entry and exit for the foreign firms, now we consider the case where the number of the foreign firms is fixed. For simplicity and without any loss of generality, we assume that there is only one foreign firm. In terms of the model specified in the previous section, we only need to disregard equation (8.6) and put $n = 1$. With these, the closed-form solutions for the key variables are

$$3\beta x_1 = \alpha - 2c_1 + c_3, \tag{8.22}$$

$$3\beta x_2 = \alpha + c_1 - 2c_3, \tag{8.23}$$

$$3p = \alpha + c_1 + c_2, \tag{8.24}$$

$$3\beta D = 2\alpha - c_1 - c_2. \tag{8.25}$$

Given these solutions, from (8.2), (8.9) and (8.10), we find

$$3\beta \frac{dW_2}{d\delta} = c_1(k_1 - k_w) > 0. \tag{8.26}$$

Equation (8.26) shows the welfare of the consuming country to be a strictly increasing function of δ. Therefore, the consuming country would always like a 100% local content restriction on the foreign firms, and, whatever the host country decides, the consuming country would ask for a more severe restriction. This result is formally stated as

Proposition 8.2 *When the number of foreign firms is exogenous, the consuming country government would always ask for a more severe local content restriction.*

We conclude this section by explaining why the behaviour of the consuming country with regard to local content restrictions could be very different when the number of foreign firms is fixed than when there is free entry and exit of foreign firms. As mentioned before, there are two broad effects of the host country's local content requirement on the consuming country's welfare, and they relate to the consumption and production sides of the economy: consumers' surplus on the one hand, and producers' surplus and wage income on the other. The effect on the consumption side is through a change in the domestic demand (D), and that on the production side is through a change in the domestic production (x_2). A more severe local content restriction harms the consumers and benefits the domestic producer. The loss to the consumers minus the gain by the domestic producer depends on a change in the difference between D and x_2, given by the total production of the foreign firms (nx_1).

In the case of free entry and exit of foreign firms, a change in local content parameter δ has no effect on x_1 and the effect on the total production of foreign firms is channelled entirely via a change in n. When the number of foreign firms is fixed, by contrast, δ affects the total production of the foreign firms only via a change in x_1. Moreover, the effect of a change in δ on n that occurs in the case of free entry and exit is much more significant than that on x_1 that occurs in the case of fixed n. To summarize, the loss to the consumers minus the gain by the domestic producer due to a more severe local content restriction is smaller for the case of a fixed number of foreign firms than for the case of free entry and exit. Therefore, the domestic producer would be treated more favourably under a fixed number of foreign firms. In particular, in this case the gain by the domestic producer dominates the loss to the consumers, and the government of the consuming country would always ask for a more severe local content restriction.

8.4   Conclusion

This chapter considered a case where foreign firms locate themselves in a host country and export their entire produce to another country, called the consuming country. The commodity is produced under an oligopolistic condition, and the foreign firms compete with a domestic firm in the consuming country. We assume the existence of unemployment in both the host and the consuming country. The host country uses a local content restriction on the foreign firms to make itself better off. In deciding the appropriate level of it there are serious conflicts of interest between the host country of FDI and the consuming country. The analysis of this conflict is at the core of this chapter.

We considered two cases depending on whether or not there is free entry and exit of foreign firms. When the number of foreign firms is endogenous, we find situations where the consuming country wants the host country to impose a less severe restriction on local contents than the host country, and vice versa.

The welfare in the host country depends entirely on the effect on employment. A more severe restriction on local contents would increase employment for a given number of foreign firms. But such a policy will also drive foreign firms away, and thus reduce employment. The host country therefore has to balance these two opposing effects in choosing an appropriate level for the local content requirement. For the consuming country, a more severe local content requirement would give the domestic firm a competitive edge, raising its profits and output, and thus employment. However, the oligopolistic distortion and therefore the price of the good would increase, reducing consumers' surplus. When, for example, the domestic firm in the consuming country is very inefficient, the interest of the consumers would dominate, and the government in the consuming country would ask for a less severe restriction on the local contents.

When the number of foreign firms is exogenous, the consuming country always wants the host country to impose a more severe restriction on local contents than the host country wants. This is because a more severe local content requirement would in this case have only a limited effect (compared to the case of free entry and exit of foreign firms) on the total production of the foreign firms.

9   Lobbying for local content requirement

9.1   Introduction

A local content regulation, viz., a restriction on the use of inputs by FDI, is clearly detrimental to the efficiency of foreign firms and this in turn is reflected in a higher price of the good and therefore a lower level of consumers' surplus, as shown in chapters 7 and 8. Why do governments, then, nevertheless impose such restrictions?

One of the main reasons for the imposition of a local content requirement is to stimulate the local economy in general and to create employment in particular. There is thus a conflict of interest between consumers on one hand and workers on the other. The government has to balance the two conflicting interests in deciding on the optimal level of the local content requirement. However, the conflict of interests also gives rise to lobbying by interest groups for a higher level of restriction on the foreign firms than otherwise would be. Therefore, in analysing local content requirements, it is imperative that one models lobbying activities explicitly.

In this chapter we consider an oligopolistic industry in which a number of foreign firms compete in the market for a non-tradeable commodity in a host country. The number of foreign firms, and hence FDI, can be affected by the host country's local content requirement. The market structure of the present model, in which the existence of any domestic firm is assumed away, is a special case of the model developed in chapter 7. However, we extend it by allowing lobbying activities.

In particular, the government is lobbied by a trade union who wants the government to stipulate that the foreign firms purchase most of their inputs from the local markets. The purpose of the lobbying activity is to maximize the income of the workers. This restriction would also affect the number of foreign firms that enter the market. We follow the approach by Grossman and Helpman (1994) in modelling the lobbying activity.[1] We assume that the trade union makes a monetary contribution to the

---

[1] Grossman and Helpman (1994) in turn apply the common agency problem, or the menu option problem, developed by Bernheim and Whinston (1986).

political party in government and the government's policy decision in turn is influenced by the amount of money it receives from the trade union.

The FDI equilibrium is specified, as in chapters 7 and 8, by equating the profits of the foreign firms to an exogenous reservation level of profits which the foreign firms could obtain if they penetrated alternative markets. Under this specification we examine how the local content restriction is determined. Among the important contributions of this chapter are the consideration of local content as a policy variable, lobbying for a strict local content requirement, and the endogeneity of the number of foreign firms.

The basic structure of the model is spelt out in detail in the following section. Section 9.3 then characterizes the political equilibrium, and section 9.4 derives properties of the optimal local content requirement. Finally, some concluding remarks are made in section 9.5.

9.2   The model

To start with we specify the model structure when no lobbying takes place. We consider an oligopolistic industry in which there are n identical foreign firms and no domestic firms.

Let k (k^f) be a foreign firm's marginal cost in the case where all inputs are bought from the host (home) country, which is assumed to be the same for all the foreign firms. As in chapter 7, we assume that

$$k > k^f \tag{9.1}$$

so that they would buy all inputs from their home country if no local content restriction is imposed. In this case, if the host country imposes local content restriction δ, the marginal cost facing the foreign firms c is given by

$$c = (1 - \delta)k^f + \delta k. \tag{9.2}$$

The n firms compete in the domestic market of a non-tradeable commodity à la Cournot. The inverse demand function for this commodity is given by

$$p = \alpha - \beta D, \quad \alpha > 0, \ \beta > 0, \tag{9.3}$$

where p and D are respectively the price and the domestic demand. Obviously, D satisfies

$$D = nx, \tag{9.4}$$

where x is a firm's output. Its profits are given by

$$\pi = (p - c)x. \tag{9.5}$$

The first-order profit maximization condition for each foreign firm is

$$p - \beta x = c. \tag{9.6}$$

The number of foreign firms n is endogenous and the government in the host country can affect this number by changing local content parameter δ. As assumed in chapters 7 and 8, the host country is small in the market for FDI and hence in equilibrium π always equals reservation profit $\bar{\pi}$ which could be earned in the rest of the world. That is,

$$\pi = \bar{\pi}. \tag{9.7}$$

This completes the description of the model structure when no lobbying takes place, and we turn now to the modelling of lobbying. For conceptual and expositional convenience we assume a complete separation between consumers and workers, i.e., the workers employed by the foreign firms do not consume the product they produce. We also assume that only the workers lobby the government and pay contributions $\lambda(\delta)$ to the government, contingent on the chosen economic policy δ. We shall discuss later how this political contribution schedule is determined.

Furthermore, since there is unemployment in the host country, the foreign firms' costs on account of domestic inputs are additional income for domestic workers. Therefore, the gross and net income of the workers, $y(\delta)$ and $\bar{y}(\delta)$ respectively, are given by

$$y(\delta) = n\delta kx, \tag{9.8}$$
$$\bar{y}(\delta) = y(\delta) - \lambda(\delta). \tag{9.9}$$

The government cares about aggregate welfare, but also about the contributions it receives from the interest group. Its objective function $V(\delta)$ is thus written as

$$V(\delta) = \theta\lambda(\delta) + W(\delta) - \lambda(\delta), \tag{9.10}$$

where θ, which is a constant parameter, is the weight the government attaches to the amount it receives for its political fund from the pressure group, and $W(\delta)$ is the aggregate welfare that could be attained in the absence of any political contribution,[2] i.e.,

$$W(\delta) = y(\delta) + CS(\delta), \tag{9.11}$$

---

[2] This particular specification implicitly assumes quasi-linear preferences for the individuals, giving rise to the constant marginal utility of income. Otherwise, one could not consider monetary transfer as equivalent to transferable utility between the government and the lobbyist, as it is done here. See Dixit, Grossman and Helpman (1997) for details.

where CS represents consumers' surplus. It is well known that

$$d\text{CS} = -Ddp. \tag{9.12}$$

We assume that

$$\theta > 1 \tag{9.13}$$

so that the government values the contributions to its political fund more than what they cost to the lobbyist.

Interactions between the pressure group, viz., the trade union, and the government decide the equilibrium levels of local content parameter δ and the political contribution schedule $\lambda(\delta)$. We now turn to the description of this interaction process and the resulting political equilibrium.

9.3   The political equilibrium

In this section we characterize the political equilibrium. As in Grossman and Helpman (1994), we consider the political equilibrium of a two-stage game in which the lobby group chooses political contribution schedule $\lambda(\delta)$ in the first stage, and the government decides on local content parameter δ in the second stage. An equilibrium is represented by political contribution schedule $\lambda(\delta)$ such that net income to the lobby group $\bar{y}(\delta)$ is maximized given the anticipated political optimization by the government in the second stage, and policy variable δ that maximizes the government's objective function $V(\delta)$, taking the political contribution schedule as given.

For the sake of brevity we do not go into the detailed description of the equilibrium (see for details Grossman and Helpman, 1994; Dixit, Grossman and Helpman, 1997). As noted by Dixit, Grossman and Helpman (1997), the model can have multiple sub-game perfect equilibria, and therefore one needs to consider further refinements of the equilibrium concept.

As in Grossman and Helpman (1994), we consider only a 'truthful' equilibrium in which the political contribution schedule has the following form:[3]

$$\lambda(\delta; z) = \text{Max}\{0, \ y(\delta) - z\}, \tag{9.14}$$

where z represents the reservation utility (to be endogenously determined). That is, a truthful contribution reflects the true welfare effect of the policy in excess of z.

---

[3] As has been shown by Bernheim and Whinston (1986), only truthful contributions support a 'coalition proof' Nash equilibrium defined as an equilibrium which is stable to non-binding communications among players.

Given political contribution schedule (9.14), the government maximizes (9.10) with respect to policy parameter δ for a given level of reservation utility z. Therefore, the optimal value of δ for this problem, which we denote δ^*, satisfies

$$\theta y'(\delta^*) + CS'(\delta^*) = 0. \tag{9.15}$$

This is the truthful equilibrium.

From (9.15) it is clear that the government implicitly maximizes a social welfare function (or, a political support function) in which the income of the trade union members is given a higher weight than the surplus due to the consumers. Moreover, the higher the value of the corruption parameter θ, the larger is the weight of the workers in the political support function.

Equation (9.15) characterizes the equilibrium value of the local content parameter. We now turn to the characterization of the equilibrium value for the political contributions by the trade union. Given the truthful contribution schedule $\lambda(\delta; z)$ in (9.14), it only remains to determine the equilibrium value of z, which is done by the requirement that the lobby group tries to pay as little as possible (i.e., tries to have as high a value for z as possible) to obtain the policy outcome as outlined above. For this to be true, given that there is only one group that lobbies, the government is indifferent between implementing the equilibrium policy and receiving the equilibrium contribution, and taking no contribution at all (Rama and Tabelini, 1998).

Defining $\hat{\delta}$ to be the optimal policy when the government receives no contribution, i.e.,

$$\hat{\delta} = \text{argmax}_\delta\ W(\delta), \tag{9.16}$$

the indifference condition states that

$$W(\hat{\delta}) = W(\delta^*) + (\theta - 1)\lambda(\delta^*;\ z), \tag{9.17}$$

where δ^* is given by (9.15). Equation (9.17) determines reservation utility z.

Grossman and Helpman (1994) have shown that both z and λ are positive in the equilibrium. If the union sets the reservation utility larger than that given by (9.17), the government would not accept the resulting contribution. That is, z given by (9.17) is the maximum utility level that the union can obtain for its members under the condition that the government would accept the contribution.[4]

---

[4] Note from (9.9) and (9.14) that in equilibrium the utility level of the trade union members is z.

This completes the characterization of the political equilibrium and in the next section we shall analyse some properties of the equilibrium.

9.4   Comparative statics

The model described in section 9.2 can be explicitly solved and some of the solutions are

$$x = \sqrt{\frac{\bar{\pi}}{\beta}},$$

$$n = \frac{\alpha - k^f - \delta(k - k^f) - \sqrt{\beta\bar{\pi}}}{\sqrt{\beta\bar{\pi}}}, \tag{9.18}$$

$$D = \frac{\alpha - k^f - \delta(k - k^f) - \sqrt{\beta\bar{\pi}}}{\beta}.$$

From (9.15), the equilibrium level of the local content parameter, δ^*, is given by

$$\delta^* = \text{argmax}_\delta \, [\bar{W}(\delta) \equiv \{\theta y(\delta) + \text{CS}(\delta)\}]. \tag{9.19}$$

Totally differentiating $\bar{W}(\delta)$ defined in (9.19) and making use of (9.8), (9.12) and (9.18) we obtain

$$\beta \frac{d\bar{W}(\delta)}{d\delta} = \{(\theta - 1)k + k^f\}\{\alpha - k^f - \sqrt{\beta\bar{\pi}}\} - \delta(k - k^f)$$
$$\times (2\theta k - k + k^f). \tag{9.20}$$

Setting $d\bar{W}/d\delta = 0$, δ^* is explicitly solved as[5]

$$\delta^* = \frac{\{(\theta - 1)k + k^f\}(\alpha - k^f - \sqrt{\beta\bar{\pi}})}{(k - k^f)(2\theta k - k + k^f)}. \tag{9.21}$$

From the above expression of δ^*, two points can be noted at once. First, even when $\theta = 1$, i.e., when the government attaches no weight to political contributions by the lobby group, the equilibrium level of δ is still strictly positive, i.e., $\delta^*|_{\theta=1} > 0$. This is because the government cares about the level of employment created by the foreign firms.

Second, the firms would not be allowed to buy any amount of inputs from abroad, i.e., $\delta^* = 1$, if

$$\theta > \frac{(k - k^f)(\alpha - k - \sqrt{\beta\bar{\pi}})}{k\{\alpha - k^f - \sqrt{\beta\bar{\pi}} - 2(k - k^f)\}}.$$

---

[5] The concavity of $\bar{W}(\delta)$ requires $2\theta k - k + k^f > 0$, which is satisfied since $\theta > 1$.

Having discussed some general properties of the equilibrium local content requirement, we shall now carry out a number of comparative static exercises. First of all, from (9.21) it follows that

$$\frac{d\delta^*}{d\bar{\pi}} < 0.$$

That is, higher reservation profits for the foreign firms imply that the local content requirement should be less stringent. This is intuitively clear. A higher value for $\bar{\pi}$ means that there would be fewer firms located in the host country which is bad for both consumers and workers. The government is therefore forced to lessen the local content requirement, encouraging more firms to locate in the host country.

We now examine the effect of a higher value for k (which could be because of a higher level of wages in the host country) on the equilibrium level of the local content requirement. From (9.21) we obtain

$$\frac{(k - k^f)\{(2\theta - 1)k + k^f\}}{\alpha - k^f - \sqrt{\beta\bar{\pi}}} \cdot \frac{d\delta^*}{dk} = -(\theta k - k + k^f)^2$$

$$-\theta\{\theta k^2 - (k - k^f)^2\} < 0.$$

That is, a higher value of local marginal cost k implies a lower value for δ^*. This result can be explained intuitively as follows. An increase in k, for a given value of δ, reduces consumers' surplus by raising the price. However, its effect on total wage income is ambiguous as it reduces the number of firms and increases the wage income generated by each firm. The government tries to redress the balance by reducing the level of δ and thus increasing the foreign firms' inflow and consumers' surplus.

Finally, we examine the effect on the equilibrium policy and contribution of a change in the 'corruption' parameter θ. From (9.21),

$$\frac{d\delta^*}{d\theta} = \frac{k(\alpha - k^f - \sqrt{\beta\bar{\pi}})}{\{(2\theta - 1)k + k^f\}^2} > 0. \tag{9.22}$$

That is, the more the government cares about the political fund it receives from the lobby group, the higher is the equilibrium level of the local content requirement. Since $\hat{\delta} = \delta^*|_{\theta=1}$ from the definition of $\hat{\delta}$ and $\theta > 1$, see (9.13), the above property implies

$$\delta^* > \hat{\delta}, \quad \text{for any } \theta \ (> 1). \tag{9.23}$$

We shall conclude this section by examining the effect of θ on the level of political distortion as measured by $W(\hat{\delta}) - W(\delta^*)$. Since x, n and p are all determined by the optimal firm behaviour and hence none of them directly depends on θ, both $W(\hat{\delta})$ and $W(\delta^*)$ are affected by θ only via its effect on the optimal levels of δ. Furthermore, $\hat{\delta}$ does not depend on θ as it is the optimal level of δ when no political contributions are accepted. Therefore, the effect of θ on the level of political distortion $W(\hat{\delta}) - W(\delta^*)$ appears only via changes in $W(\delta^*)$. Since $\delta^* > \hat{\delta}$ (see (9.23)) and $\partial W/\partial\delta|_{\delta=\hat{\delta}} = 0$ from the definition of $\hat{\delta}$, the concavity of $W(\delta)$ implies $\partial W/\partial\delta|_{\delta=\delta^*} < 0$. This property and (9.22) prove that a rise in θ decreases $W(\delta^*)$ and thus increase political distortion $W(\hat{\delta}) - W(\delta^*)$.

9.5 Conclusion

Foreign penetration through foreign direct investment (FDI) creates new job opportunities and thereby benefits workers. However, if the foreign firms hire inputs from their home countries, the job-creation effect weakens. Thus, trade unions have an incentive to lobby the government so that the latter imposes a local content restriction on FDI and urges the foreign firms to hire more local inputs. Therefore, political economic considerations must be at the heart of an analysis which tries to examine the determinant of local content restrictions.

FDI has another effect, namely the price-lowering effect, making consumers better off. Therefore, local content restrictions, which reduce the incentive of foreign firms to enter the host country, lower consumers' surplus. It causes a conflict of interest between consumers and workers. In determining the optimal level of the local content requirement the government has to balance the conflicting interests.

In this chapter, we have developed a model of FDI which explicitly treats an endogenous lobbying process. We then characterized the political equilibrium in which the level of local content requirement and political contributions are simultaneously determined. One of our results is that a country with a higher wage level has a less stringent local content requirement. However, a higher political corruption in the host country implies a stricter local content requirement.

We conclude by noting certain limitations of our analysis. First of all, we do not allow international trade, and thus foreign firms do not have the option of exporting the commodity rather than establishing a firm in the host country. Second, we consider the case of linear demand. Third, we only have one interest group. Fourth, we do not allow the government to consider other instruments such as profit taxation in dealing with the foreign firms.

10 Foreign direct investment in the presence of cross-hauling

10.1 Introduction

The inflow of foreign firms and the outflow of domestic firms at the same time – the phenomenon of cross-hauling – is a well-founded empirical fact. There are many Japanese automobile firms located in the USA and at the same time there are many US firms that are located in, for example, Europe. In the international trade theory this phenomenon was first investigated by Caves (1971) and later on by Amano (1977) and Jones, Neary and Ruanne (1983). However, they considered foreign investment of the portfolio type, and, to our knowledge, no one has considered the cross-hauling of FDI.

In this chapter we consider an oligopolistic market in which a number of domestic and foreign firms produce two non-tradeable differentiated commodities. Both the number of domestic firms and that of foreign firms are affected by the government of the host country with the use of lump-sum subsidies to the domestic and foreign firms. The basic model developed here extends that of chapter 7 by endogenizing the number of domestic firms. As in chapter 7, the FDI equilibrium is specified by equating each firm's profits to an exogenous reservation level of profits which it could obtain if it penetrated an alternative market.

In this setting we examine the effect of discriminatory and uniform subsidies on the inflow/outflow of domestic and foreign firms and on the level of employment. We also find the properties of the optimal subsidies. Among the important contributions of this chapter are to allow for the number of domestic and foreign firms to be endogenous and for the cross-hauling of domestic and foreign firms to occur, none of which can be found in the literature.

After presenting the basic structure of the model in the following section, we discuss the effect of both discriminatory and uniform subsidies on employment in section 10.3. Section 10.4 derives the properties of the optimal subsidies. We consider subsidies that discriminate between domestic and foreign firms as well as those that do not. Section 10.5 concludes.

128

10.2   The model

We consider a market in which there are m identical domestic firms and n identical foreign firms. The marginal costs of the domestic and foreign firms are c and c^f respectively. These marginal costs are taken to be constant, and therefore they are also the average variable costs.

The domestic and the foreign firms produce two imperfectly substitutable commodities. Demand for a domestic (or foreign) product is represented by D (or D^f) and the price of a domestic (foreign) product by p (or p^f). The utility function of a representative consumer is

$$u(D, D^f) = \alpha D + \alpha^f D^f - \frac{\beta D^2 + \beta^f (D^f)^2 + 2\gamma DD^f}{2} + y,$$

$$(10.1)$$

where γ is a parameter representing the degree of product differentiation satisfying

$$\beta > \gamma > 0 \quad \text{and} \quad \beta^f > \gamma > 0, \tag{10.2}$$

and y is the consumption of the numeraire good. From (10.1), the inverse demand functions are derived as

$$p = \alpha - \beta D - \gamma D^f, \tag{10.3}$$
$$p^f = \alpha^f - \beta^f D^f - \gamma D. \tag{10.4}$$

Since the commodities are non-tradeable, we have

$$D = mx, \quad D^f = nx^f, \tag{10.5}$$

where x and x^f are respectively the output of a domestic and that of a foreign firm. They earn profits π and π^f respectively and these are given by

$$\pi = (p - c)x + S, \tag{10.6}$$
$$\pi^f = (p^f - c^f)x^f + S^f, \tag{10.7}$$

where S and S^f are the lump-sum subsidies given to each domestic and foreign firm respectively.[1]

There are M domestic firms, m of which operate in the host country and $M - m$ are located abroad. The number of foreign firms n and the number of domestic firms m operating in the host country are endogenous and the government of the host country affects these numbers by changing the values of subsidies S and S^f. Since the host country is assumed to

---

[1] As in chapter 7, we assume that the tax is source based rather than residence based, and that the home government does not tax firms on subsidies received abroad.

be small in the market for FDI, the domestic and foreign firms move in and out of the host country so that in equilibrium π^f and π equal the respective reservation profits $\bar{\pi}^f$ and $\bar{\pi}$, i.e.,

$$\pi^f = \bar{\pi}^f, \quad \pi = \bar{\pi}. \tag{10.8}$$

The firms – domestic and foreign – are assumed to behave in a Cournot-Nash fashion, and therefore the first-order profit maximization conditions are

$$p - \beta x = c, \tag{10.9}$$
$$p^f - \beta^f x^f = c^f. \tag{10.10}$$

Since there is unemployment in the host country, the variable input costs of the firms are added to the host country's surplus. Therefore, labour income E (which we shall call 'employment' since E divided by a given unit wage is actually the employment level) and welfare W of the representative consumer are respectively

$$E = mcx + nc^f x^f, \tag{10.11}$$
$$W = M\bar{\pi} - nS^f - mS + E + CS, \tag{10.12}$$

where the second and the third terms in (10.12) are the subsidy payments, the first term is the profits of the domestic firms, and CS is consumers' surplus. Obviously, a change in CS satisfies

$$dCS = -Ddp - D^f dp^f. \tag{10.13}$$

10.3 Comparative statics

In this section we analyse the effects of changes in the lump-sum subsidies to foreign (S^f) and domestic firms (S) on the inflow/outflow of both types of firms and also on the level of employment in the host country. Turning first to the question of inflow/outflow, we obtain the following (see appendix F for the derivation in detail):

$$dm = \frac{\sqrt{\bar{\pi}^f - S^f}\{(m+1)\beta\beta^f - m\gamma^2\}dS - \gamma\sqrt{\beta\beta^f}(\bar{\pi} - S)dS^f}{\sqrt{\bar{\pi}^f - S^f}(\bar{\pi} - S)(\beta\beta^f - \gamma^2)}, \tag{10.14}$$

$$dn = \frac{\sqrt{\bar{\pi} - S}\{(n+1)\beta\beta^f - n\gamma^2\}dS^f - \gamma\sqrt{\beta\beta^f}(\bar{\pi}^f - S^f)dS}{\sqrt{\bar{\pi} - S}(\bar{\pi}^f - S^f)(\beta\beta^f - \gamma^2)}. \tag{10.15}$$

Equations (10.14) and (10.15) under assumption (10.2) immediately imply that an increase in S^f raises n and lowers m. Thus, a discriminatory policy does lead to the phenomenon of cross-hauling in the present model. The intuition is fairly straightforward. For example, an increase in the subsidy to foreign firms raises their profits encouraging more foreign firms to flow in. However, more foreign firms make the markets more competitive reducing the profits of each domestic and foreign firm. This leads to the outflow of domestic firms.

Turning to the effect of subsidies on the level of employment, E, we obtain (see appendix F for the derivation)

$$dE = \frac{\sqrt{(\bar{\pi}-S)\beta^f}(\beta c^f - \gamma c)dS^f + \sqrt{(\bar{\pi}^f - S^f)\beta}(\beta^f c - \gamma c^f)dS}{2\sqrt{(\bar{\pi}-S)(\bar{\pi}^f - S^f)}(\beta\beta^f - \gamma^2)}.$$

$$(10.16)$$

From (10.16) we observe that when γ is zero so that the two products are completely differentiated, subsidies to the firms of any group unambiguously raise the level of employment. This is because in the absence of any interdependence between the two sets of firms (i.e., $\gamma = 0$) subsidies to the firms of one group have no effect on the number of firms in the other group (see (10.14) and (10.15)). Subsidies to the firms of one group raise their profits, which encourages them to enter the country more, and therefore to increase the level of employment. However, the subsidies do not cause cross-hauling because of the absence of interdependence.

At the other extreme, i.e., when the goods are nearly homogeneous $(\gamma \simeq \beta = \beta^f)$, subsidies to the firms of one group raise employment if and only if the firms of that group are less efficient than those of the other group. This is because in our framework less efficient firms create more employment per unit of output. For example, subsidizing the foreign firms creates new employment by attracting more foreign firms, but it also reduces employment by driving some of the domestic firms out of the country. The net effect is positive if the foreign firms are less efficient and thus employ more labour. Formally,

Proposition 10.1 *Subsidies to the firms of one group, but not to the firms of the other, cause cross-hauling. Subsidizing the foreign firms, but not the domestic ones, increases employment if and only if $c^f > c\gamma/\beta$. Similarly, subsidizing the domestic firms, but not the foreign ones, increases employment if and only if $c > c^f\gamma/\beta^f$.*

So far we have only considered discriminatory subsidies, i.e., subsidies either to the foreign firms or to the domestic firms, but not to both. We now consider the effect of uniform subsidies to both the domestic and foreign firms. To start with, assume that $\bar{\pi} = \bar{\pi}^f$ and $S = S^f = \bar{S}$ (say).

With these assumptions, equations (10.14)–(10.16) reduce to

$$\frac{dm}{d\bar{S}} = \frac{(m+1)\beta\beta^f - m\gamma^2 - \gamma\sqrt{\beta\beta^f}}{(\bar{\pi} - \bar{S})(\beta\beta^f - \gamma^2)}$$

$$\frac{dn}{d\bar{S}} = \frac{(n+1)\beta\beta^f - n\gamma^2 - \gamma\sqrt{\beta\beta^f}}{(\bar{\pi} - \bar{S})(\beta\beta^f - \gamma^2)},$$

$$\frac{dE}{d\bar{S}} = \frac{\left(\sqrt{\beta^f\beta} - \gamma\right)\left(c^f\sqrt{\beta} + c\sqrt{\beta^f}\right)}{2\sqrt{(\bar{\pi} - \bar{S})}(\beta\beta^f - \gamma^2)}.$$

In view of (10.2), the above three equations imply that uniform subsidies to both the domestic and foreign firms raise the number of both of them, and increase employment. Formally,

Proposition 10.2 *Equal subsidies to domestic and foreign firms increase the number of both firms and the level of employment if $\bar{\pi} = \bar{\pi}^f$.*

When $\bar{\pi} \neq \bar{\pi}^f$, there is a case where uniform entry-promoting subsidies $\bar{S}$ actually reduce employment. To prove this we rewrite (10.16) for the case of uniform subsidies as

$$\frac{dE}{d\bar{S}} = \frac{c^f\left[\beta\sqrt{\beta^f(\bar{\pi} - \bar{S})} - \gamma\sqrt{\beta(\bar{\pi}^f - \bar{S})}\right] + c\left[\beta^f\sqrt{\beta(\bar{\pi}^f - \bar{S})} - \gamma\sqrt{\beta^f(\bar{\pi} - \bar{S})}\right]}{2\sqrt{(\bar{\pi} - \bar{S})(\bar{\pi}^f - \bar{S})}(\beta\beta^f - \gamma^2)}.$$

(10.17)

From (10.17) we obtain two alternative sufficient conditions for the uniform subsidies to reduce the level of employment, and these are: (1) $c \simeq 0$, $\bar{\pi} < \bar{\pi}^f\gamma^2/(\beta\beta^f)$, and (2) $c^f \simeq 0$, $\bar{\pi}^f < \bar{\pi}\gamma^2/(\beta\beta^f)$. The first set of conditions states that the domestic firms do not create much employment and their reservation profit level is relatively small (and therefore they are relatively numerous). Similarly, the second set of conditions states that the foreign firms do not create much employment and they are relatively numerous. That is, uniform subsidies reduce employment if there are many firms in one of the two groups and they create much employment. Formally,

Proposition 10.3 *Equal subsidies to domestic and foreign firms reduce employment if either (1) $c \simeq 0$, $\bar{\pi} < \bar{\pi}^f\gamma^2/(\beta\beta^f)$, or (2) $c^f \simeq 0$, $\bar{\pi}^f < \bar{\pi}\gamma^2/(\beta\beta^f)$.*

10.4   Optimal subsidies

Having examined the effects of the subsidies on the inflow/outflow of firms and on employment, in this section we shall analyse the welfare effects. The main welfare equation is derived as (see (F.10.19) in appendix F)

$$xx^f \theta \, dW = [a_1 S + a_2 S^f + a_3] \, dS + [b_1 S + b_2 S^f + b_3] \, dS^f, \tag{10.18}$$

where

$$\theta = xx^f \beta\beta^f (\beta\beta^f - \gamma^2) > 0,$$
$$a_1 = -\beta^f (x^f)^2 \{\beta\beta^f (m+1) - m\gamma^2\} < 0,$$
$$a_2 = b_1 = \gamma\beta\beta^f xx^f > 0,$$
$$a_3 = x^f \theta D + \beta\beta^f x(x^f)^2 (\beta^f c - \gamma c^f),$$
$$b_2 = -\beta x^2 \{\beta\beta^f (n+1) - n\gamma^2\} < 0,$$
$$b_3 = x\theta D^f + \beta\beta^f x^2 x^f (\beta c^f - \gamma c).$$

We shall first consider a discriminatory policy; namely, subsidizing the foreign firms and not the domestic ones.[2] In particular, we shall examine the effect of increasing subsidies S^f to the foreign firms when there are not initial subsidies, i.e., $S = S^f = 0$.

From (10.18), we find

$$x^f \left. \frac{\partial W}{\partial S^f} \right|_{S=S^f=0} = D^f + \frac{\beta c^f - \gamma c}{\beta\beta^f - \gamma^2}. \tag{10.19}$$

Equation (10.19) shows that subsidizing the foreign firms has two effects on welfare. First, it brings in more foreign firms, increasing competition and therefore reducing prices. The welfare-enhancing effect of the price reduction is given by the first term on the right-hand side of (10.19). The second term is the employment effect. As mentioned before, this effect can be either positive or negative. If the employment effect is positive then the effect on welfare is also positive. Moreover, assuming the welfare function to be concave with respect to S^f, it is found that the optimal level of S^f is positive if $\beta c^f - \gamma c > 0$. Formally,

Proposition 10.4 *In the absence of any policy towards the domestic firms, the optimal level of the subsidy to the foreign firms is positive if $\beta c^f - \gamma c > 0$.*

The above proposition obviously does not rule out the possibility of a tax on FDI. However, the proposition implies that a necessary condition for a tax on FDI is that the employment effect is negative, i.e.,

---

[2] The analysis for the other case, i.e., when the domestic firms are subsidized and the foreign ones are not is similar and therefore omitted.

$\beta c^f - \gamma c < 0$. We shall now obtain a sufficient condition under which the optimal policy is to tax FDI.

As is shown in appendix F, D^f can be solved as (see (F.10.9) in appendix F)

$$D^f = \frac{-\beta\sqrt{\beta^f(\bar{\pi}^f - S^f)} + \beta^f(\alpha^f - c^f) + \gamma\sqrt{\beta(\bar{\pi} - S)} - \gamma(\alpha - c)}{\beta\beta^f - \gamma^2}.$$

(10.20)

Substituting the value of D^f from (10.20) into (10.19) we find

$$(\beta\beta^f - \gamma^2)x^f \left.\frac{dW}{dS^f}\right|_{S=S^f=0} = -\beta\sqrt{\beta^f\bar{\pi}^f} + \gamma\sqrt{\beta\bar{\pi}}$$

$$+ \beta^f\alpha^f + (\beta - \beta^f)c^f - \gamma c. \quad (10.21)$$

From (10.20) and (10.21), it is clear that $dW/dS^f < 0$ if $\bar{\pi}^f >> \bar{\pi}$ and $c >> c^f$. That is, when there are many small labour-intensive domestic firms and a few large labour-saving foreign firms, discouraging FDI by taxing them is the optimal policy. An example which fits these conditions is the retailing industry in many countries which is often dominated by numerous small 'firms' – the so-called 'corner' shops. In such situations, our result suggests that the country should not encourage the entrance of a few large and efficient foreign 'supermarkets'. Formally,

Proposition 10.5 *In the absence of any policy towards the domestic firms, the optimal policy is to tax the foreign firms if $c >> c^f$ and $\bar{\pi} << \bar{\pi}^f$.*

Having obtained a property of the optimal subsidy to the foreign firms when no policies are applied to the domestic firms, we shall now consider simultaneous but discriminatory applications of subsidies to both the domestic and foreign firms. Setting the coefficients of both dS and dS^f in (10.18) to zero and solving for S and S^f, we obtain the optimal values for the two subsidies as

$$\hat{S} = \frac{\beta x[D\{(n+1)\beta\beta^f - n\gamma^2\} + \beta^f\gamma D^f + \{\beta^f c + n(\beta^f c - \gamma c^f)\}]}{\Delta},$$

(10.22)

$$\hat{S}^f = \frac{\beta^f x^f[D^f\{(m+1)\beta\beta^f - m\gamma^2\} + \beta\gamma D + \{\beta c^f + m(\beta c^f - \gamma c)\}]}{\Delta},$$

(10.23)

where $\Delta = \beta\beta^f(m + n + mn + 1) - mn\gamma^2 > 0$.

The first two terms in the expressions for the optimal subsidies are positive and these appear because of the price-lowering effect of the subsidies. That is, the subsidies to the firms of one group encourage more of them to come into the country, reducing the degree of monopoly and thus the prices. The third term appears because of the employment effect. Using (10.16), we note that the third term in the expression for $\hat{S}^f$ (or $\hat{S}$) is also positive if $\partial E/\partial S^f > 0$ (or $\partial E/\partial S > 0$). Formally,

Proposition 10.6 *When discriminatory subsidies to domestic and foreign firms are simultaneously determined, the optimal subsidy to the foreign (domestic) firms is positive if $\beta c^f - \gamma c > 0$ ($\beta^f c - \gamma c^f > 0$).*

Once again, the above proposition establishes a sufficient condition for each optimal subsidy to be positive. We shall now derive sufficient conditions for it to be negative. Clearly, from the above proposition, a necessary condition for the optimal policy to be a tax, rather than a subsidy, is that the subsidy reduces employment. We shall only examine the case where $\hat{S}^f$ is negative: the analysis for $\hat{S}$ will be similar.

We begin by introducing a few more notations. First, the welfare function is denoted by $W(S, S^f)$. Second, we denote by $\hat{S}(S^f)$ the optimal value for S for a given value of S^f. From (10.18), it is clear that $\hat{S}(S^f)$ is a solution of

$$a_1 \hat{S}(S^f) + a_2 S^f + a_3 = 0. \tag{10.24}$$

Also from (10.18), we note that

$$\hat{S}^f < 0 \quad \text{if} \quad xx^f\theta \left. \frac{dW(\hat{S}(S^f), S^f)}{dS^f} \right|_{S^f=0} = b_1 \hat{S}(0) + b_3 < 0.$$

Using the value of $\hat{S}(0)$ from (10.24), those of a_i and b_i ($i = 1, 2, 3$) given in (10.18), and that of D^f given by (10.20), we obtain

$$\lambda (x^f)^2 \sqrt{\beta^f} (\beta\beta^f - \gamma^2) \cdot \left. \frac{dW(\hat{S}(S^f), S^f)}{dS^f} \right|_{S^f=0}$$

$$= \lambda \left(-\beta\sqrt{\beta^f\bar{\pi}^f} + \beta^f\alpha^f - \gamma\alpha + \gamma\sqrt{\beta(\bar{\pi} - \hat{S}(0))} \right) + \gamma\sqrt{\beta(\bar{\pi} - \hat{S}(0))}$$

$$\times \left(-\beta^f\sqrt{\beta(\bar{\pi} - \hat{S}(0))} + \beta(\alpha - c) + \gamma\sqrt{\beta^f\bar{\pi}^f} - \gamma\alpha^f + \beta^f c \right), \tag{10.25}$$

where

$$\lambda = \beta(\alpha - c) - \gamma(\alpha^f - c^f) + \gamma\sqrt{\beta^f\bar{\pi}^f}$$
$$= x^f\{(\beta\beta^f - \gamma^2)m + \beta\beta^f\} > 0.$$

Equation (10.25) implies that

$$\hat{S}^f < 0 \quad \text{if } \bar{\pi} - \hat{S}(0) \simeq 0 \text{ and } \beta\sqrt{\beta^f \bar{\pi}^f} > \beta^f \alpha^f - \gamma\alpha. \quad (10.26)$$

Let us examine when the conditions in (10.26) are valid. From (F.10.7), we find

$$\bar{\pi} - \hat{S}(0) = 0 \quad \Longleftrightarrow \quad x = 0. \quad (10.27)$$

Moreover, from (10.24) and the definitions of θ, a_1 and a_3 given in (10.18), we have

$$\hat{S}(0) = -a_3/a_1 = [(\beta\beta^f - \gamma^2)D$$
$$+ (\beta^f c - \gamma c^f)]x\beta/\{\beta\beta^f(m+1) - m\gamma^2\},$$

which implies

$$\hat{S}(0) = 0 \quad \Longleftrightarrow \quad x = 0. \quad (10.28)$$

Therefore, from (10.27) and (10.28), we obtain

$$\bar{\pi} - \hat{S}(0) = 0 \quad \Longleftrightarrow \quad \bar{\pi} = 0. \quad (10.29)$$

Equations (10.26) and (10.29) imply

Proposition 10.7 *When discriminatory subsidies to domestic and foreign firms are simultaneously determined, the optimal subsidy to the foreign firms is negative if $\bar{\pi} \simeq 0$ and $\beta\sqrt{\beta^f \bar{\pi}^f} > \beta^f \alpha^f - \gamma\alpha$.*

The conditions mean that there are numerous domestic firms and a small number of foreign firms. In this situation it is optimal to tax the foreign firms.

Finally, we analyse the case where a uniform subsidy is applied to both groups. In this case, its optimal level is obtained by equating the sum of the coefficients of dS and dS^f to zero and solving for $\bar{S} (= S = S^f)$. Thus,

$$\hat{\bar{S}} = \frac{x^f \theta D + x\theta D^f + \beta\beta^f x(x^f)^2(\beta^f c - \gamma c^f) + \beta\beta^f x^2 x^f(\beta c^f - \gamma c)}{\beta^f(x^f)^2\{\beta\beta^f(m+1) - m\gamma^2\} + \beta x^2\{\beta\beta^f(n+1) - n\gamma^2\} + 2\beta\beta^f xx^f\gamma}. \quad (10.30)$$

The denominator in the right-hand side of (10.30) is positive. The first and the second terms in the numerator are positive and represent the price-lowering effect of the subsidy. The third and the fourth terms are there due to the employment effect on the domestic and foreign firms respectively (see (10.16)). When $\bar{\pi} = \bar{\pi}^f$, the sum of the third and the fourth term becomes $(\bar{\pi} - \bar{S})^{\frac{3}{2}}(c\sqrt{\beta^f} + c^f\sqrt{\beta})(\sqrt{\beta\beta^f} - \gamma)$, which is positive.

This result is formally stated as

Proposition 10.8 *When a uniform subsidy is applied to both domestic and foreign firms, the optimal level of the subsidy is positive when* $\bar{\pi} = \bar{\pi}^f$.

10.5   Conclusion

As FDI grows rapidly all over the world, the phenomenon of cross-hauling, where the inflow of foreign firms and the outflow of domestic firms take place at the same time, becomes more and more popular. Therefore, when formulating policies on FDI a government cannot ignore, as they often do, the effects that the policies may have on domestic firms. Otherwise, many of the domestic firms will simply vote with their feet to the detriment of the local economy.

In this chapter we have developed a theoretical model of an economy which is small in the international market for FDI and in which domestic firms are also internationally mobile. Under this framework, we first examined the effect of both discriminatory and uniform subsidy policies towards foreign and domestic firms on the level of employment in the host country. We find that subsidizing the foreign firms, but not the domestic firms, may reduce employment because of the outflow of the domestic firms. A uniform subsidy does not have such consequences if both groups of firms face the same level of reservation profits. Otherwise, even the uniform subsidy may reduce employment. We also examined properties of the optimal discriminatory and uniform subsidies and find that it may not always be optimal to subsidize FDI.

Appendix F

Totally differentiating (10.6) and (10.7) and using (10.8), (10.9) and (10.10), we find

$$-\beta x dx + \beta x dD + \gamma x dD^f = dS,\qquad\text{(F.10.1)}$$
$$-\beta^f x^f dx^f + \beta^f x^f dD^f + \gamma x^f dD = dS^f.\qquad\text{(F.10.2)}$$

Multiplying (F.10.1) by m and using (10.5), we have

$$(m-1)\beta x dD + mx\gamma dD^f = mdS - \beta x^2 dm.\qquad\text{(F.10.3)}$$

Similarly, multiplying (F.10.2) by n and using (10.5), we get

$$(n-1)\beta^f x^f dD^f + nx^f \gamma dD = ndS^f - \beta(x^f)^2 dn.\qquad\text{(F.10.4)}$$

Substituting (10.3)–(10.5) into (10.9) and (10.10) and totally differentiating the results we derive

$$m\gamma dD^f + (m+1)\beta dD = \beta x dm,$$ (F.10.5)

$$n\gamma dD + (n+1)\beta^f dD^f = \beta^f x^f dn.$$ (F.10.6)

From (10.6)–(10.10),

$$\sqrt{\beta}x = \sqrt{\bar{\pi} - S}, \quad \sqrt{\beta^f}x^f = \sqrt{\bar{\pi}^f - S^f}.$$ (F.10.7)

Substituting (10.3), (10.4) and (F.10.7) into (10.9) and (10.10) and then solving for D and D^f, we obtain

$$D = \frac{-\beta^f\sqrt{\beta(\bar{\pi} - S)} + \beta(\alpha-c) + \gamma\sqrt{\beta^f(\bar{\pi}^f - S^f)} - \gamma(\alpha^f - c^f)}{\beta\beta^f - \gamma^2},$$ (F.10.8)

$$D^f = \frac{-\beta\sqrt{\beta^f(\bar{\pi}^f - S^f)} + \beta^f(\alpha^f - c^f) + \gamma\sqrt{\beta(\bar{\pi} - S)} - \gamma(\alpha - c)}{\beta\beta^f - \gamma^2}.$$ (F.10.9)

Solving the four equations (F.10.3)–(F.10.6) for dD, dD^f, dm and dn, and using (F.10.7) we find

$$dD = \frac{\sqrt{\beta^f\beta(\bar{\pi}^f - S^f)}dS - \gamma\sqrt{\bar{\pi} - S}dS^f}{2\sqrt{\bar{\pi} - S}x^f(\beta\beta^f - \gamma^2)},$$ (F.10.10)

$$dD^f = \frac{\sqrt{\beta\beta^f(\bar{\pi} - S)}dS^f - \gamma\sqrt{\bar{\pi}^f - S^f}dS}{2x\sqrt{\bar{\pi}^f - S^f}(\beta\beta^f - \gamma^2)},$$ (F.10.11)

$$dm = \frac{\sqrt{\bar{\pi}^f - S^f}\{(m+1)\beta\beta^f - m\gamma^2\}dS - \gamma\sqrt{\beta\beta^f(\bar{\pi} - S)}dS^f}{\sqrt{\bar{\pi}^f - S^f}(\bar{\pi} - S)(\beta\beta^f - \gamma^2)},$$ (F.10.12)

$$dn = \frac{\sqrt{\bar{\pi} - S}\{(n+1)\beta\beta^f - n\gamma^2\}dS^f - \gamma\sqrt{\beta\beta^f(\bar{\pi}^f - S^f)}dS}{\sqrt{\bar{\pi} - S})(\bar{\pi}^f - S^f)(\beta\beta^f - \gamma^2)}.$$ (F.10.13)

Differentiation of (F.10.7) gives

$$dx = -\frac{dS}{2\beta x},$$ (F.10.14)

$$dx^f = -\frac{dS^f}{2\beta^f x^f}.$$ (F.10.15)

Totally differentiating (10.11) and using (F.10.7) and (F.10.12)–(F.10.15), we get

$$dE = \frac{\sqrt{(\bar{\pi} - S)\beta^f}(\beta c^f - \gamma c)dS^f + \sqrt{(\bar{\pi}^f - S^f)}\beta(\beta^f c - \gamma c^f)dS}{2\sqrt{(\bar{\pi} - S)(\bar{\pi}^f - S^f)}(\beta\beta^f - \gamma^2)}.$$

(F.10.16)

From (10.3), (10.4), (F.10.10) and (F.10.11), we obtain

$$dp = -\frac{dS}{2x},$$

(F.10.17)

$$dp^f = -\frac{dS^f}{2x^f}.$$

(F.10.18)

Finally, differentiating (10.12) and substituting the above equations into the result, one obtains

$$
\begin{aligned}
x^2(x^f)^2\beta\beta^f(\beta\beta^f - \gamma^2)\, dW = & \left[-S\beta^f(x^f)^2\{\beta\beta^f(m+1) - m\gamma^2\}\right. \\
& + \gamma\beta\beta^f xx^f S^f + \beta\beta^f x(x^f)^2 D(\beta\beta^f - \gamma^2) \\
& \left. + \beta\beta^f x(x^f)^2(\beta^f c - \gamma c^f)\right] dS \\
& + \left[-S^f\beta x^2\{\beta\beta^f(n+1) - n\gamma^2\} + \gamma\beta\beta^f xx^f S\right. \\
& + \beta\beta^f x^2 x^f D^f(\beta\beta^f - \gamma^2) \\
& \left. + \beta\beta^f x^2 x^f(\beta c^f - \gamma c)\right] dS^f.
\end{aligned}
$$

(F.10.19)

Bibliography

Agarwal, M. and A. Barua, 1994, Effects of entry in a model of oligopoly with international trade, *Journal of International Trade and Economic Development*, 3, 1–14.

Amano, A., 1977, Specific factors, comparative advantage and international investment, *Economica*, 44, 131–44.

Asplund, M. and R. Sandin, 1999, The number of firms and production capacity in relation to market size, *Journal of Industrial Economics*, 47, 69–85.

Bagwell, K. and Staiger, R. W., 1994, The sensitivity of strategic and corrective R&D policy in oligopolistic industries, *Journal of International Economics*, 36, 133–50.

Baldwin, R. E., 1960, The effect of tariffs on international and domestic prices, *Quarterly Journal of Economics*, 74, 65–78.

Barry, F. and J. Bradly, 1997, FDI and trade: the Irish host-country experience, *Economic Journal*, 107, 1778–811.

Bergsten, C. F., T. Horst and T. H. Moran, 1978, *American multinationals and American interests* (Washington D.C.: Brookings Institute).

Bernheim, B. and M. Whinston, 1986, Menu auctions, resource allocation, and economic influence, *Quarterly Journal of Economics*, 101, 1–31.

Bernhofen, D. M., 1998, Intra-industry trade and strategic interaction: theory and evidence, *Journal of International Economics*, 45, 77–96.

Besley, T. and K. Suzumura, 1992, Taxation and welfare in an oligopoly with strategic commitment, *International Economic Review*, 33, 413–31.

Bhagwati, J. N., 1971, The generalized theory of distortions and welfare, in: J. N. Bhagwati, R. W. Jones, R. A. Mundell and J. Vanek, eds., *Trade, balance of payments, and growth: papers in international economics in honor of Charles P. Kindleberger* (Amsterdam: North-Holland).

Bhagwati, J. N. and H. G. Johnson, 1961, A generalized theory of the effect of tariffs on the term of trade, *Oxford Economic Papers*, 13, 225–53.

Bhagwati, J. N. and V. K. Ramaswamy, 1963, Domestic distortions, tariffs and the theory of optimum subsidy, *Journal of Political Economy*, 71, 44–50.

Bhattacharjee, A., 1995, Strategic tariffs and endogenous market structures: trade and industrial policies under imperfect competition, *Journal of Development Economics*, 47, 287–312.

Brander, J. A., 1981, Intra-industry trade model in identical commodities, *Journal of International Economics*, 11, 1–14.

1995, Strategic trade policy, in G. M. Grossman and K. Rogoff, eds., *Handbook of international economics*, vol. 3 (Amsterdam: North-Holland), pp. 1395–456.

Brander, J. A. and P. R. Krugman, 1983, A reciprocal dumping model of international trade, *Journal of International Economics*, 15, 313–21.

Brander, J. A. and B. J. Spencer, 1983, Strategic commitment with R&D: the symmetric case, *Bell Journal of Economics*, 14, 225–35.

1984, Tariff protection and imperfect competition, in H. Kierzkowski, ed., *Monopolistic competition and international trade* (Oxford: Clarendon Press).

1985, Export-subsidies and international market share rivalry, *Journal of International Economics*, 18, 83–100.

1987, Foreign direct investment with unemployment and endogenous taxes and tariffs, *Journal of International Economics*, 22, 257–79.

Bulow, J. I., J. D. Geanakoplos and P. D. Klemperer, 1985, Multimarket oligopoly: strategic substitutes and complements, *Journal of Political Economy*, 93, 488–511.

Caho, C. and E. S. H. Yu, 1997, Trade liberalization in oligopolistic competition with unemployment: a general equilibrium analysis, *Canadian Journal of Economics*, 30, 479–96.

Casson, M. and R. Pearce, 1987, Multinational enterprises in LDCs, in N. Gemmel and S. Ghatak, eds., *Surveys in development economics* (Oxford: Basil Blackwell) ch. 3.

Caves, R., 1971, International corporations: the industrial economics of foreign investment, *Economics*, 38, 1–27.

Choe, C., 1999, Retail and wholesale margins in successive Cournot oligopolies, *Australian Economic Papers*, 38, 1–8.

Collie, D. R., 1998, Trade policy under Bertrand duopoly with integrated markets: the pure strategy equilibrium, *Economic Letters*, 60, 179–83.

Cordella, T., 1998, Pattern of trade and oligopoly equilibria: an example, *Review of International Economics*, 6, 554–63.

Cordella, T. and J. J. Gabszewicz, 1997, Comaparative advantage under oligopoly, *Journal of International Economics*, 43, 333–46.

Corden, W. M., 1974, *Trade policy and economic welfare* (Oxford: Clarendon Press).

d'Aspremont, C. and A. Jacquemin, 1988, Cooperative and noncooperative R&D in duopoly with spillovers, *American Economic Review*, 78, 1133–7.

Davidson, C., S. J. Matusz and M. E. Kreinin, 1985, Analysis of performance standards for direct foreign investment, *Canadian Journal of Economics*, 101, 876–90.

Delipalla, S. and M. J. Keen, 1992, The comparison between *ad valorem* and specific taxation under imperfect competition, *Journal of Public Economics*, 49, 351–67.

Denicolò, V. and M. Matteuzzi, 2000, Specific and ad valorem taxation in asymmetric Cournot oligopolies, *International Tax and Public Finance*, 7, 335–44.

Devereux, M. and R. Griffith, 1996, Taxes and location of production: evidence from a panel of US multinationals, presented at the TAPES conference organised by the National Bureau of Economic Research.

Dick, A. R., 1993, Strategic trade policy and welfare: the empirical consequences of cross-ownership, *Journal of International Economics*, 35, 227–49.

Dixit, A. K., 1984, International trade policies for oligopolistic industries, *Economic Journal*, 94, 1–16.

1986, Comparative statics for oligopoly, *International Economic Review*, 27, 107–22.

Dixit, A., G. M. Grossman and E. Helpman 1997, Common agency and co-ordination: general theory and application to tax policy, *Journal of Political Economy*, 105, 752–69.

Dixon, H. D., 2001, Oligopoly theory made simple, in *Surfing economics: essays for the inquiring economist* (London: Palgrave), ch. 6, pp.125–60.

Doyle, C. and S. van Wijnbergen, 1994, Taxation of foreign multinationals: a sequential bargaining approach to tax holidays, *International Tax and Public Finance*, 1, 211–26.

Dunning, J. H., 1993, *Multinational enterprises and the global economy* (Working-ham: Addison-Wesley).

Eaton, J. and G. M. Grossman, 1992, Optimal trade and industrial policy under oligopoly, in G. M. Grossman, ed., *Imperfect competition and international trade* (Cambridge, Mass.: MIT Press), pp. 121–40.

Ethier, W. J., 1986, The multinational firm, *Quarterly Journal of Economics*, 101, 805–33.

Ethier, W. J. and H. Horn, 1990, Managerial control of international firms and the pattern of direct investment, *Journal of International Economics*, 28, 25–45.

Fine, B., 1999, Competition and market structure reconsidered, *Metroeconomica*, 50, 194–218.

Friedman, J., 1983, *Oligopoly theory* (New York: Cambridge University Press).

Fung, K. C., 1995, Rent shifting and rent sharing: a re-examination of the strategic industrial policy problem, *Canadian Journal of Economics*, 28, 450–62.

Gatsion, K. and L. Karp, 1992, The welfare effects of imperfect harmonisation of trade and industrial policy, *Economic Journal*, 102, 107–16.

Gisser, M. and R. D. Sauer, 2000, The aggregate relation between profits and concentration is consistent with Cournot behaviour, *Review of Industrial Organization*, 16, 229–50.

Glass, A. J. and K. Saggi, 1999, FDI policies under shared factor markets, *Journal of International Economics*, 49, 309–32.

Greaney, T. M., 1999, Manipulating market shares: the indirect effects of volun-tary import expansion, *Japan and the World Economy*, 11, 95–113.

Grossman, G. M., 1981, The theory of domestic content protection and content preference, *Quarterly Journal of Economics*, 96, 583–603.

Grossman, G. M. and E. Helpman, 1994, Protection for sale, *American Economic Review*, 84, 833–54.

Hahn, F. H., 1962, The stability of the Cournot oligopoly solution, *Review of Economic Studies*, 29, 329–31.

Hamilton, S. F. and K. Stiegert, 2000, Vertical coordination, antitrust law and international trade, *Journal of Law and Economics*, 43, 143–56.

Haskel, J. and P. Scaramozzino, 1997, Do other firms matter in oligopolies?, *Journal of Industrial Economics*, 45, 27–46.

Haufler, A., 2001, *Taxation in a global economy* (New York: Cambridge University Press).

Haufler, A. and G. Schjelderup, 2000, Corporate tax systems and cross country profit shifting, *Oxford Economic Papers*, 52, 306–25.

Haufler, A. and I. Wooton, 1999, Country size and tax competition for foreign direct investment, *Journal of Public Economics*, 71, 121–39.

Helpman, E., 1984a, Increasing returns, imperfect markets, and trade theory, in R. W. Jones and P. B. Kennen, eds., *Handbook of international economics*, vol. 1 (Amsterdam: North-Holland), pp. 325–65.

1984b, A simple theory of international trade with multinational corporations, *Journal of Political Economy*, 92, 451–71.

Helpman, E., and P. Krugman, 1986, *Market structure and foreign trade* (Cambridge, Mass.: MIT Press).

1989, *Trade policy and market structure* (Cambridge, Mass.: MIT Press).

Helpman, E. and A. Razin, 1983, Increasing returns, monopolistic competition, and factor movements, *Journal of International Economics*, 14, 263–76.

Herander, M. and Thomas, C., 1986, Export performance and export–import linkage requirements, *Quarterly Journal of Economics*, 51, 591–607.

Hillman, A. and H. Ursprung, 1993, Multinational firms, political competition and international trade policy, *International Economic Review*, 34, 347–63.

Holm, P., 1997, Vertically integrated oligopoly and international trade policy, *Canadian Journal of Economics*, 30, 194–207.

Hood, N. and S. Young, 1979, *The economics of multinational enterprise* (London: Longman).

Hortsmann, I. J. and J. R. Markusen, 1986, Up the average cost curve: inefficient entry and new protectionism, *Journal of International Economics*, 20, 225–48.

1987, Strategic investments and the development of multinationals, *International Economic Review* 28, 109–21.

1992, Endogenous market structures in international trade (natura facit saltum), *Journal of International Economics*, 32, 109–29.

Hwang, H. S. and C. T. Schulman, 1993, Strategic non-intervention and the choice of trade policy for international oligopoly, *Journal of International Economics*, 34, 73–93.

Hymer, S., 1972, The international corporation and the law of uneven development, in J. Bhagwati, ed., *Economics and world order* (New York: Macmillan), pp. 113–40.

1976, *The international operations of national firms: a study of direct foreign investment* (Cambridge, Mass.: MIT Press).

IMF (International Monetary Fund), 1996, *International capital markets, developments, prospects, and key policy issues* (Washington, D.C.: International Monetary Fund).

Ishikawa, J. and B. J. Spencer, 1999, Rent-shifting export subsidies with an imported intermediate product, *Journal of International Economics*, 48, 199–232.

Janeba, E., 1995, Corporate income tax competition, double taxation and foreign direct investment, *Journal of Public Economics*, 56, 311–25.

Johnson, H. G., 1954–5, Optimal tariffs and retaliation, *Review of Economic Studies*, 22, 142–53.

Jones, R., 1974, The Metzler tariff paradox, in G. Horwich and P. A. Samuelson, eds., *Trade, stability and macroeconomics* (New York: Academic).

Jones, R. W., P. J. Neary and F. Ruanne, 1983, Two way capital flows: cross-hauling in a model of foreign investment, *Journal of International Economics*, 14, 357–66.

Katrak, Homi, 1977, Multinational monopolies and commercial policy, *Oxford Economic Papers*, 29, 283–91.

Katz, M. and C. Shapiro, 1985, On the licencing of innovation, *Rand Journal of Economics*, 16, 504–20.

Katz, M. L., 1986, An Analysis of Cooperative Research and Development, *Rand Journal of Economics*, 17, 527–43.

Keen, Michael, 1991, Corporation tax, foreign direct investment and the single market, in L. A. Winters and A. J. Venables, eds., *European integration: trade and industry* (Cambridge University Press), pp. 164–98.

Kemp, M. C., 1967, Notes on the theory of optimal tariffs, *Economic Record*, 43, 395–403.

Klette, T. J., 1994, Strategic trade policy for exporting industries: more general results in the oligopolistic case, *Oxford Economic Papers*, 46, 296–310.

Kojima, K., 1990, Industrial policy under international oligopoly, *Kobe Economic and Business Review*, 35, 69–76.

Komiya, R., M. Okuno and K. Suzumura (eds.), 1988, *Industrial policy of Japan* (San Diego: Academic Press).

Kreps, D. and J. Scheinkman, 1983, Quantity precommitment and Bertrand competition yield Cournot outcome, *Bell Journal of Economics*, 14, 326–37.

Krishna, K. and M. Itoh, 1988, Content protection and oligopolistic interactions, *Review of Economic Studies*, 55, 107–25.

Krugman, P. R., 1979, Increasing returns, monopolistic competition and international trade, *Journal of International Economics*, 9, 469–80.

Krugman, P. R. and M. Obstfeld, 1994, *International economics: theory and practice* (New York: HarperCollins College Publishers).

Krugman, P. R. and A. Smith eds., 1994, *Empirical studies of strategic trade policy* (Chicago: University of Chicago Press).

Lahiri, S. and Y. Ono, 1988, Helping minor firms reduces welfare, *Economic Journal*, 98, 1199–202.

1995a, Elimination of firm and welfare under international oligopoly, in W. Chang and S. Katayama, eds., *Imperfect competition and international trade* (Boston: Kluwer Academic Press), Chapter 7.

1995b, The role of free entry in an oligopolistic Heckscher–Ohlin model, *International Economic Review*, 36, 609–24.

1997, Asymmetric oligopoly, international trade and welfare: a synthesis, *Journal of Economics*, 65, 291–310.

1998a, Foreign direct investment, local content requirement, and profit taxation, *Economic Journal*, 108, 444–57.

1998b, Tax policy on foreign direct investment in the presence of cross-hauling, *Weltwirtschaftliches Archiv*, 134, 263–79.

1999a, Optimal tariffs in the presence of middlemen, *Canadian Journal of Economics*, 32, 55–70.

1999b, R&D subsidies under asymmetric duopoly: a note, *Japanese Economic Review*, 50, 118–125.

2003, Export-oriented foreign direct investment and local content requirement, *Pacific Economic Review*, 8, 1–14.

Leahy, D. and C. Montagna, 2001, Strategic trade policy with heterogeneous costs, *Bulletin of Economic Research*, 53, 177–82.

Leahy, D. and J. P. Neary, 2000, Strategic trade and industrial policy towards dynamic oligopolies, *Economic Journal*, 110, 484–508.

2001, Robust rules for industrial policy in open economies *Journal of International Trade and Economic Development*, 10, 393–409.

Lopez-de-Silanes, F., J. R. Markusen and T. F. Rutherford, 1996, Trade policy subtleties with multinational firms, *European Economic Review*, 40, 1605–28.

Long, N. van and A. Soubeyran, 1997, Cost heterogeneity, industry concentration and strategic trade policies, *Journal of International Economics*, 43, 207–20.

Maggi, G., 1996, Strategic trade policies with endogenous mode of competition, *American Economic Review*, 86, 237–58.

Markusen, J. R. and A. J. Venables, 1988, Trade policy with increasing returns and imperfect competition: contradictory results from competing assumptions, *Journal of International Economics*, 24, 299–316.

Metzler, L., 1949, Tariffs, international demand and domestic prices, *Journal of Political Economy*, 57, 345–51.

Motta, M., 1992, Multinational firms and the tariff jumping argument: a game theoretic analysis with some unconventional conclusions, *European Economic Review*, 36, 1557–71.

Myles, G. D., 1996, Imperfect competition and the optimal combination of *ad valorem* and specific taxation, *International Tax and Public Finance*, 3, 29–44.

Neary, J. P., 1988, Export subsidies and price competition, *Empirica-Austrian Economic Papers*, 15, 243–61.

1994, Cost asymmetries in international subsidy games: should governments help winners or losers?, *Journal of International Economics*, 37, 197–218.

Norman, G. and M. LaManna, eds., 1992, *The new industrial economics – recent developments in industrial organization, oligopoly and game theory* (Aldershot: Edward Elgar).

Okuno-Fujiwara, M. and K. Suzumura, 1993, Symmetric Cournot oligopoly and economic welfare: a synthesis, *Economic Theory*, 3, 43–59.

Ono, Y., 1978, The equilibrium of duopoly in a market of homogeneous goods, *Economica*, 45, 287–95.

1982, Price leadership: a theoretical analysis, *Economica*, 49, 11–20.

1990, Foreign penetration and national welfare under oligopoly, *Japan and the World Economy*, 2, 141–54.

Petit, M. L. and F. SannaRandaccio, 2000, Endogenous R&D and foreign direct investment in international oligopolies, *International Journal of Industrial Organization*, 18, 339–76.

Qiu, L. D. and Z. Tao, 2001, Export foreign direct investment, and local content requirement, *Journal of Development Economics*, 66, 101–25.

Rama, M. and G. Tabelini, 1998, Lobbying by capital and labor over trade and labor market policies, *European Economic Review*, 42, 1295–316.

Richardson, M., 1991, The effect of content requirement on a foreign duopsonist, *Journal of International Economics*, 31, 143–55.

   1993, Content protection with foreign capital, *Oxford Economic Papers*, 24, 103–17.

Riley, J., 1970, Ranking of tariffs under monopoly power in trade: an extension, *Quarterly Journal of Economics*, 84, 710–12.

Rowthorn, R. E, 1992, Intra-industry trade and investment under oligopoly – the role of market size, *Economic Journal*, 102, 402–14.

Ruffin, R. J., 1977, Cournot oligopoly and competitive behavior, *Review of Economic Studies*, 38, 493–502.

   1984, International factor movements, in R. W. Jones and P. B. Kenen, eds., *Handbook of international economics*, vol. 1 (Amsterdam: North-Holland), pp. 237–88.

Schmalensee, R., 1976, Is more competition necessarily good?, *Industrial Organization Review*, 4, 120–1.

Scitovsky, T., 1949, A reconsideration of the theory of tariffs, *Review of Economic Studies*, 9, 89–110.

Seade, J., 1980, On the effects of entry, *Econometrica*, 48, 479–89.

Smith, A., 1987, Strategic investment, multinational corporations and trade policy, *European Economic Review*, 31, 89–96.

Spence, M., 1984, Cost reduction, competition, and industry performance, *Econometrica*, 52, 101–22.

Spencer, B. J. and J. A. Brander, 1983, International R&D rivalry and industrial strategy, *Review of Economic Studies*, 50, 707–22.

Stiglitz, J. E., 1981, Potential competition may reduce welfare, *American Economic Review*, Papers and Proceedings, 71, 184–9.

Suzumura, K., 1992, Cooperative and non-cooperative R&D in an oligopoly with spillovers, *American Economic Review*, 82, 1307–20.

   1995, *Competition, commitment and welfare* (Oxford: Clarendon Press).

Suzumura, K. and K. Kiyono, 1987, Entry barriers and economic welfare, *Review of Economic Studies*, 54, 157–67.

Tanaka, Y., 1992, Welfare effects of tariffs in free-entry oligopoly under integrated markets, *Economic Studies Quarterly*, 43, 210–29.

Tandon, P., 1984, Innovation, market structure and welfare, *American Economic Review*, 74, 394–403.

Tirole, J., 1988, *The theory of industrial organization* (Boston, Mass.: MIT Press).

Tugendhat, C., 1971, *The multinationals* (Harmondsworth: Penguin Books).

UNIDO, 1986, *Industrial policy and the developing countries: an analysis of local content regulations.* UNIDO/IS.606, 3 February.

Ushio, Y., 2000, Welfare effects of commodity taxation in Cournot oligopoly, *Japanese Economic Review*, 51, 268–73.

Varian, H., 1995, Entry and cost reduction, *Japan and the World Economy*, 7, 399–418.

Venables, A. J., 1985, Trade and trade policy with imperfect competition: the case of identical products and free entry, *Journal of International Economics* 19, 1–19.

Vernon, R., 1971, *Sovereignty at bay* (New York: Basic Books).

Viner, J., 1937, *Studies in the theory of international trade* (London: George Allen and Unwin).

von Weizsäcker, C. C., 1980a, A welfare analysis to barriers to entry, *Bell Journal of Economics*, 11, 399–420.

1980b, *Barriers to entry: a theoretical treatment* (Berlin: Springer Verlag).

Wildasin, D., 1989, Interjurisdictional capital mobility: fiscal externality and a corrective subsidy, *Journal of Urban Economics*, 25, 296–315.

Yabuuchi, S., 1997, Direct investment, monopoly and welfare, *Pacific Economic Review*, 2, 135–45.

Index